Bible Brain Builders, Volume 4

Other Bible Brain Builders

Bible Brain Builders

Volume 4

THOMAS NELSON

Since 1798

NASHVILLE   DALLAS   MEXICO CITY   RIO DE JANEIRO

Published in Nashville, Tennessee, by Thomas Nelson. Thomas Nelson is a registered trademark of Thomas Nelson, Inc.

Book design and composition by Graphic World, Inc.

Original puzzles and mazes created by W. B. Freeman.

Thomas Nelson, Inc., titles may be purchased in bulk for educational, business, fund-raising, or sales promotional use. For information, please e-mail SpecialMarkets@ThomasNelson.com.

The material in this book originally was published in other forms in *Nelson's Super Book of Bible Word Games, Book 1,* © 1992, *Nelson's Super Book of Bible Word Games, Book 2,* © 1993, *Nelson's Super Book of Bible Word Games, Book 3,* © 1993, *Incredible Mazes, Book 1,* © 1993, *Incredible Mazes, Book 2,* © 1994 by Thomas Nelson Publishers, Inc., all rights reserved.

Unless otherwise noted, Scripture quotations are taken from THE NEW KING JAMES VERSION. © 1982 by Thomas Nelson, Inc. Used by permission. All rights reserved.

Verses marked KJV are taken from the HOLY BIBLE: KING JAMES VERSION

Verses marked NIV are taken from the HOLY BIBLE: NEW INTERNATIONAL VERSION®. © 1973, 1978, 1984 by International Bible Society. Used by permission of Zondervan Publishing House. All rights reserved.

ISBN: 978-1-4185-4915-2

Printed in Mexico

14 13 12 11 QG 1 2 3 4 5 6

STAYING LIT

*M*atthew 5:16 says, "Let your light so shine before men, that they may see your good works and glorify your Father in heaven." This candle has a breeze shield that allows the user to protect the flame from wind drafts.

The Holy Spirit both lights the flame of our light and provides us with protection against the winds of the enemy who tries to extinguish our light for the Lord.

A number of life-changing events for Bible personalities took place "in the field" or out in the countryside. Find the names of twelve of these Bible people in the letter grid below. (One of the "names" is a title, two words.)

```
L B A N O S O J U R V D C A A I A N P
E U T E G Y A I T N I S N A A I T I T
G J O W I L F C I D O S A L V I D I S
Y A H M A N D S H E S A E G Y M P T A
P S E S M A A C A D A B A L A A M I U
J F P J T H R U R A S E B N H N A A C
O I H O O B A E N B G L A A I O A N B
N W E S U N H H A Y H E P D L A L S A
A H C E R P A T P D E H C A A H C B A
D O A P E H C T A I R S C B T S P A L
A A I H R T I N H V D L I U I W E A J
V M S U L A S O D A S A R D D I S C O
M A A D N U A J C D N B A A M F O I N
A N B A E L A H P E S V N O J E J S A
N O E V I A C S A J I O N A T H A R W
O A S A A C B A A C I W N A M H T U I
H R U T D A V I J O S E A E B A F G C
R L A B S I C A A C E B L G Y P N I A
```

Scripture Pool
GENESIS 4:8; 24:63; 37:13–15   NUMBERS 22:23   JUDGES 13:9   RUTH 2:2–3
1 SAMUEL 11:5; 16:11–13 19:2–3; 30:11   LUKE 2:8

*T*o keep … to follow … to obey. As Christians, we are admonished to keep the commandments, follow the leading of the Spirit, and "obey God rather than men" (Acts 5:29). Put together the two halves of these "obedience" verses and match each verse with its Scripture citation.

Column A

1. But God be thanked that though you were slaves of sin,

2. Since you have purified your souls in obeying the truth through the Spirit in sincere love of the brethren,

3. For as by one man's disobedience many were made sinners,

4. You shall walk after the LORD your God and fear Him,

5. Has the LORD as great delight in burnt offerings and sacrifices,

6. If anyone loves Me, he will keep My word;

7. Obey My voice, and I will be your God, and you shall be My people.

Column B

A. and My Father will love him, and We will come to him and make Our home with him.

B. and keep His commandments and obey His voice; you shall serve Him and hold fast to Him.

C. yet you obeyed from the heart that form of doctrine to which you were delivered.

D. And walk in all the ways that I have commanded you, that it may be well with you.

E. so also by one Man's obedience many will be made righteous.

F. as in obeying the voice of the LORD?

G. love one another fervently with a pure heart.

Column C

Deuteronomy 13:4

Romans 5:19

1 Peter 1:22

Jeremiah 7:23

John 14:23

1 Samuel 15:22

Romans 6:17

Column A	Column B	Column C
1	___	___
2	___	___
3	___	___
4	___	___
5	___	___
6	___	___
7	___	___

As you complete the words of Isaiah 55 below, you'll have all the clues you need to finish the crossword!

"_____! Everyone who _____, come to the
70 Across   10 Across

_____; and you who have no _____, come,
4 Down   51 Down

_____ and _____ . _____, come, buy _____
72 Across   5 Down   48 Across   4 Across

and _____ without money and without _____ .
12 Down   3 Down

Why do you _____ money for what is not
20 Across

bread, and your wages for what does not

satisfy? _____ carefully to _____, and eat
78 Across   77 Down

what is good, and let your soul _____ itself in
34 Down

_____ . _____ your _____, and come to _____ .
9 Across 44 Across   60 Down   15 Across

Hear, and your _____ shall live; and I will
41 Across

make an _____ _____ with you—the sure
13 Across 58 Across

_____ of David. Indeed I have given him as a
33 Down

_____ to the people, a _____ and _____ for the
75 Across   8 Down   27 Down

people. Surely you shall call a nation you do

not know, and _____ who do _____ know you
45 Down   61 Across

shall run to you, because of the Lord your

_____, and the _____ One of Israel; for He
56 Down   65 Across

has glorified _____ ."
76 Down

_____ the Lord _____ He may be _____,
17 Across   49 Down   1 Down

_____ _____ Him while He is near. Let the
74 Down 55 Down

wicked _____ his _____, and the _____ _____
46 Down   36 Across   79 Across 63 Across

his thoughts; let him _____ to the Lord, and
2 Down

He will have mercy _____ him; _____ to our
16 Across   6 Down

God, for He will abundantly _____ .
73 Across

"_____ My thoughts _____ not your _____,
1 Across   38 Across   43 Down

nor are your ways My _____," says the _____ .
11 Down   32 Down

"For as the heavens are _____ than the earth,
53 Across

_____ are My ways higher _____ your ways,
54 Across   26 Down

and My thoughts than your _____ ."
62 Down

"For as the _____ comes down, and the snow
7 Down

from _____, and do not return there, but
40 Down

_____ the _____, and make it bring forth and
71 Down   69 Down

_____, _____ _____ may give _____ to the
39 Down 52 Down 42 Across   35 Across

_____ and bread to the _____, so shall _____
68 Across   21 Down   63 Down

word be that goes _____ from My _____; it
23 Across   47 Across

shall not return to Me _____, but it shall
14 Down

_____ what I _____, and it shall _____ in the
59 Down   57 Across   67 Down

_____ for which I _____ it.
64 Down   22 Down

"For _____ shall go out with _____, and be led
19 Down   18 Across

out with peace; the _____ and the _____ shall
51 Across   24 Down

break forth into singing before you, and all the

trees of the _____ shall _____ their hands.
23 Down   30 Across

Instead of the _____ shall come up the _____
28 Across   25 Down

tree, and instead of the _____ shall come
37 Across

_____ the _____ _____ ; and it shall be _____
66 Across 31 Across 29 Across   50 Across

the Lord for a name, for an everlasting sign

that shall not be _____ off."
25 Across

St. Andrew's Cross

*T*his cross shape has a number of other names, such as Cross Saltire, St. Patrick's Cross, the Scottish Cross, St. Alban's Cross, and Crux Decussata.

According to church tradition, the apostle Andrew died on this form of cross. Feeling himself unworthy to be crucified on the same type of cross as that on which his Lord, Jesus Christ, had died, he requested that the form of his cross be different. Tradition states that he died in prayer, just as Jesus did.

This emblem is frequently used as part of liturgical garments that are worn on St. Andrew's Day, November thirtieth.

As a silver cross on a blue background, this cross shape is the national cross of Scotland. When used as a symbol for St. Patrick, the cross is colored red.

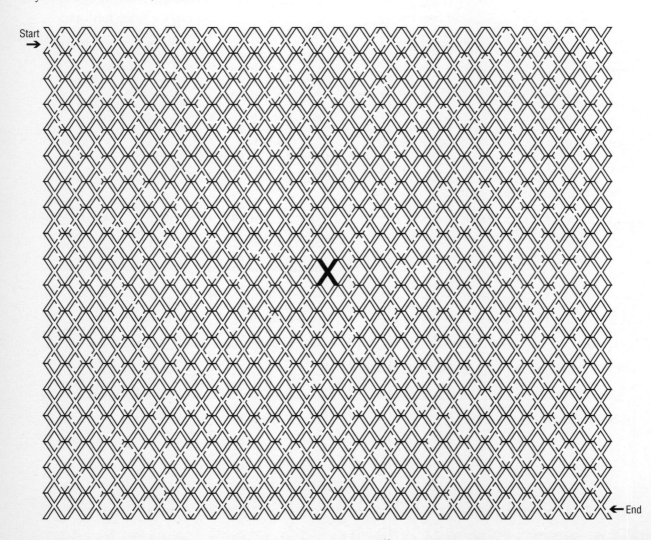

*T*he words below are related in the Scriptures to one of the most frequently used analogies for material and spiritual prosperity. As you unscramble the words—and then fit them onto the grid below—you will discover the name of the one who watches over and takes care of this blessing.

OEWNR   UNRPE
ETDN   ARPGES
UFRIT   INVE
MSOSLOBS   SLCUETSR
NBARCHSE   SERKEPE
SICDPEWNIE (2 words)

```
        V I N E
      F R U I T
        T E N D
      K E E P E R S
    S P I C E D   W I N E (2 words)
        B R A N C H E S
      O W N E R
      C L U S T E R S
    B L O S S O M S
    P R U N E
      G R A P E S
```

VINEDRESSER

Scripture Pool
LEVITICUS 25:3   SONG OF SOLOMON 7:12; 8:2, 11–12   JEREMIAH 8:13
MATTHEW 20:8   JOHN 15:1, 4–5   REVELATION 14:18

*A*ll of the clues to this crossword begin with the letter *N*. See how many you can answer before looking up the Scripture references.

Across

2 The time of day Nicodemus came to Jesus (John 3:1–2)

3 Jesus raised a widow's only son from death in this city (Luke 7:11–15)

6 He was called a "mighty hunter before the LORD" (Genesis 10:9)

7 Commander of the Syrian king's army, he became a leper and was cured by dipping seven times in the Jordan River (2 Kings 5:1–14)

8 The Lord told Jonah to "cry out against" this wicked city (Jonah 1:1–2)

10 Hannah prayed, "No one is holy like the LORD, for there is _____ besides You" (1 Samuel 2:2)

11 King of Babylon, he built a golden image of himself and insisted that the people bow down and worship it or be thrown in a fiery furnace (Daniel 3:1–6)

12 In John's revelation, those who serve the beast have _____ rest (Revelation 14:11)

14 Deborah was the name of Rebekah's _____ (Genesis 35:8)

15 Servant of King Artaxerxes, he rebuilt the walls of Jerusalem (Nehemiah 1)

16 John had a vision of an angel having the everlasting gospel to preach to those of "every _____, tribe, tongue, and people" (Revelation 14:6)

18 John wrote, "Let him who has understanding calculate the _____ of the beast, for it is the _____ of a man: His _____ is 666" (Revelation 13:18)

20 Jesus told the disciples to "cast the _____ on the right side of the boat" to catch fish (John 21:6)

21 "Let us therefore come boldly to the throne of grace, that we may obtain mercy and find grace to help in time of _____" (Hebrews 4:16)

22 Joshua's father (Joshua 1:1)

24 The psalmist described the rebuke of the LORD as "the blast of the breath of Your _____" (Psalm 18:15)

26 Abram had two brothers: _____ and Haran (Genesis 11:26)

27 The disciple whom Jesus saw "under the fig tree" (John 1:45–51)

Down

1 Thomas said he would not believe Jesus was resurrected unless he saw and touched "in His hands the print of the _____" (John 20:25)

2 Ruth's mother-in-law (Ruth 1:3–4)

3 Obadiah wrote, "The day of the LORD upon all the nations is _____" (Obadiah 15)

4 One of the first seven men chosen to take care of the "ministry business" of the early church (Acts 6:5)

5 The prophet who advised King David (2 Samuel 7:1–17)

8 The Lord showed Moses the land of promise from the top of this mountain (Deuteronomy 34:1–4)

9 Called "a ruler of the Jews," it was to him that Jesus said, "Unless one is born again, he cannot see the kingdom of God" (John 3:1–3)

10 Jesus' hometown (John 1:45)

11 Called "the city of the priests," it was attacked by Doeg the Edomite (1 Samuel 22:18–19)

13 Paul wrote that Jesus Christ is above "every name that is _____" (Ephesians 1:21)

15 Jesus healed the son of "a certain _____man" in Capernaum (John 4:46–53)

17 Jesus said that it is "easier for a camel to go through the eye of a _____ than for a rich man to enter the kingdom of God" (Matthew 19:24)

19 The name of the first month of the year on the Jewish calendar (Esther 3:7)

21 Abigail's first husband (1 Samuel 25:3)

23 Builder of the ark (Genesis 6:13–14)

24 The name of the thirty-fourth book of the Bible

25 Either, or; neither, _____

Some of the answers to this petal puzzle are people or things God uses to prophesy; some of the other answers are the fulfillment of prophecies. Solve the puzzle as you would a crossword, working clockwise and counterclockwise instead of "down and across." The first clockwise answer is provided as an example.

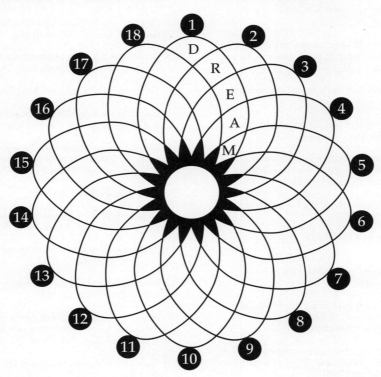

Clockwise

1 "Old man's" prophetic tool
2 Pulsating ache
3 West Point trainee
4 Concrete, steady
5 Luxurious fur animal
6 Summit or toothpaste
7 Lubricated
8 Tale or legend
9 Last's opposite
10 Morning bread slice
11 Large sea mammal
12 Category
13 Some will wear his mark (Revelation 13:16–17)
14 Hum, buzz
15 Thrill, exhilarate
16 Wine and jelly source
17 Snatches
18 People of the "Emerald Isle"

Counterclockwise

1 Swag window covering
2 Israel had twelve of these (sing.)
3 "Royal" board game
4 Prophecy of a son made her laugh
5 A city whose doom was foretold
6 Israelite general of note
7 Trajectory
8 As prophesied, Judas's thirty pieces of silver bought the potter's _____
9 The Bible warns *against* _____ prophets
10 Yak's home
11 God so loved the _____
12 Pursue
13 Explosion
14 Bargained or dispensed
15 Wipe out
16 Sheen
17 Endowment
18 Angry

JACOB'S RETURN

*I*n Genesis 25, we find the story of two brothers so different that conflict was the constant theme of their life together. Esau, the elder brother, was his father Isaac's favorite son. Large and bronzed from his days hunting in the fields, Esau is described as hairy. He was probably considered a "man's man." As the older brother, he was more than likely a take-charge man which fit him well since he had the right to inherit all his father's holdings.

But the younger brother Jacob was his mother's favorite and he spent his days doing as she instructed him. By using these skills along with his mother's cunning and determination to secure the inheritance for her favorite son, Jacob was able to cheat Esau out of his birthright. As a result Jacob had to flee for his life and spent many years exiled from his family.

Jacob wants to return to his father's tent without being killed by his angry brother Esau. Armed with a bow and arrow, Esau can see all the way to the end of each path where he stands, but he can see only in the direction in which he is looking. He cannot see the paths that cross over or under the path he is on.

*T*he Bible has a number of stories about people who gave to others—either freewill gifts or tribute. Find the names of twelve of these "givers" in the box of letters below. See how many you can find before consulting the Scripture Pool.

```
N M O A B J E H T M A R J R C Z T
E H O R I T S O O I H S E U Z R H
B W L Y T A H A T A S E B A I S A
U I N S O S B P H A B H O P I H D
C D E P E I W R O R N E S H E E N
H A M I T C N C A I L E S Z C B M
A M E E I H E S U H T R W Z O A O
D S S O R H B E J T A Z I A R N A
N H I M I Z U M E T I M D R N E B
E A W M P T A H P A H S O H E J S
Z P W N S O E L I W R P W O L Z E
Z H A E I D N Z Z U C I S C I T B
A M M O N I T E S O A B I O U Y I
R A T N C O R E N M S E T R S W S
E M D A H C U B T U I L E N D I E
```

Scripture Pool

GENESIS 25:6   2 SAMUEL 8:2   1 KINGS 10:10   2 CHRONICLES 21:1–3; 26:8
PSALM 72:10   DANIEL 2:1, 6, 48   MATTHEW 2:1,11   LUKE 21:1–4
ACTS 10:1–2   1 CORINTHIANS 12:4, 7

Caleb, Israel's mighty military leader, has an important meeting with Moses in the tent at the center of the maze. On the way, however, he must pass *through* twenty of his captain's tents without passing through any part of the maze twice.

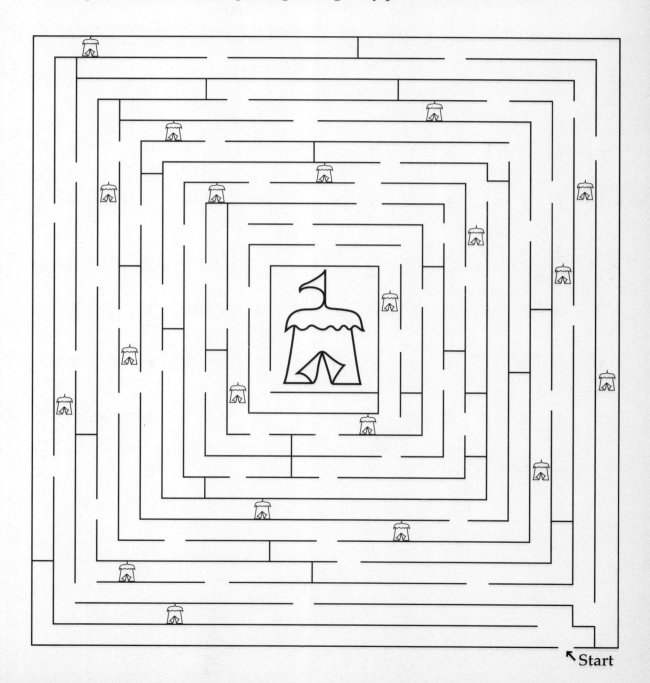

↖ Start

*F*ind an important message in the box of letters below, and when you do, circle the letters that spell out the message!

X   Y   Z   U   Z   Y   Y   Z   U   Z   U   X   U   X   Y   Z

U   I   T   I   Z   U   S   X   G   Y   O   Y   R   E   C   U

Y   S   Z   Y   X   X   E   Y   I   X   T   Z   E   Y   Z   X

Z   M   U   E   S   U   D   Z   V   U   N   U   I   V   X   Z

U   O   X   L   Z   Z   T   U   E   T   A   X   E   U   Z   U

X   R   E   B   Z   Y   O   X   Y   H   Z   Y   ACTS 20:35

Z   Y   U   X   Y   X   Z   Z   U   X   Y   Z   U   X   Y   Z

*E*verything old was new again, when Jesus said, "It is written . . ."

Across

1 The rejected stone became the "main" cornerstone (Matthew 21:42)

6 Israel will say to these "small mountains," "Cover us!" (Luke 23:30)

7 Whoever commits this will be in danger of judgment (Matthew 5:21)

9 Science fiction (abbr.)

13 "A man's enemies will be those of his own 'home'" (Matthew 10:36)

15 Each (abbr.)

16 Isaiah said the people honored God with their "mouths," but not their hearts (Mark 7:6)

17 Road (abbr.)

18 If this sibling won't make amends, confront him with two or three witnesses (Matthew 18:15–16)

20 Jesus cited the "abomination of desolation" spoken of by this prophet (Matthew 24:15)

21 God desires this, not sacrifice (Matthew 9:13)

23 Like

24 Doctor (abbr.)

25 Judas ate this with Jesus, then betrayed Him (John 13:18)

26 They hated Him without a "reason" (John 15:25)

27 A house of prayer became a _____ of thieves (Matthew 21:13)

Down

2 The corpses of unrepentant sinners: Their "flame" is not quenched (Mark 9:48)

3 These members of the flock were scattered (Matthew 26:31)

4 "And the two shall become one _____" (Matthew 19:5)

5 "And He was numbered with the 'sinners'" (Luke 22:37)

8 Man doesn't live by this alone (Matthew 4:4)

10 Echoing David, Jesus asked, "Why have You _____ Me?" (Matthew 27:46)

11 "Respect" your father and mother (Matthew 15:4)

12 Looking on a woman with lust is the same as committing this, Jesus said (Matthew 5:27–28)

14 Satan couldn't tempt Jesus to "wait on" him instead of God (Matthew 4:10)

18 David was the first to say, "Out of the mouth of _____" (Matthew 21:16)

19 He *is* — not *was*— the God of Abraham, Isaac, and _____ (Matthew 22:32)

21 In the beginning, He "created" them male and female (Matthew 19:4)

22 God couldn't "restore" the people whose ears and eyes were closed (Matthew 13:15)

24 The hearts of the people, as Isaiah prophesied, had grown "blunt" (Matthew 13:15)

*R*eady for a mountaintop experience? Find the names of sixteen mountains named in the Bible. (See how many you can find before consulting the Word Pool.)

```
G  Z  I  O  L  I  B  A  L  I  G  O  B  H  B  A
I  S  O  S  B  E  O  D  E  A  M  E  R  O  N  L
L  E  N  I  A  T  A  A  B  E  D  T  L  I  A  E
B  V  L  N  R  H  L  O  M  O  R  I  A  S  I  B
A  I  A  A  E  O  I  A  V  S  G  O  I  G  O  L
L  C  R  L  C  R  C  R  E  G  E  R  I  Z  I  M
E  B  I  O  A  E  L  M  I  Z  A  R  E  P  V  S
A  G  C  L  M  B  E  L  A  I  G  B  Z  I  A  R
L  A  A  I  S  S  E  I  R  L  O  D  R  S  P  E
R  I  R  V  E  A  B  A  A  B  A  E  A  G  I  P
M  O  M  N  D  I  N  M  R  D  A  A  N  A  G  I
P  I  E  O  L  S  E  R  A  O  L  O  N  H  M  R
E  Z  L  I  R  O  B  A  T  V  M  B  M  E  N  O
R  A  O  Z  A  I  L  Z  S  R  A  L  A  B  B  M
A  L  M  C  R  M  A  I  E  E  N  I  Z  I  G  O
M  B  R  O  L  E  N  H  V  S  I  G  T  E  T  H
E  E  A  M  E  A  L  E  M  E  S  B  A  S  A  E
R  A  H  N  I  S  A  D  O  R  S  O  R  H  R  R
A  E  R  I  O  L  I  G  L  I  A  C  I  A  S  M
T  E  V  R  L  C  M  O  I  Z  V  E  R  O  R  O
```

Word Pool

ARARAT CARMEL EBAL GERIZIM GILBOA GILEAD HERMON
HOREB MORIAH NEBO OLIVES PISGAH SEIR SINAI TABOR ZION

THE RETURN HOME

*T*he life of the prodigal son that Jesus told about in a parable in Luke 15:11–32, is filled with difficult twists and turns. The young son pressured his father for his inheritance and then set out on a wild life of pleasure and excess that cost him everything he had inherited.

The young son was lost in his waywardness as his wanderings led him to the "pits" of the pig sty. There he determined to return home to become his father's sevant. But instead of servanthood, he was welcomed back by his father with a great feast as a beloved son. The older son, who had conducted his life in a much wiser manner, was angered by the celebration and confronted his father. The father declared that nothing had been taken away from the older son and everything that the father had belonged to him. What had been dead was now alive, and what was lost had been found. And so the father rejoiced.

Start ↓

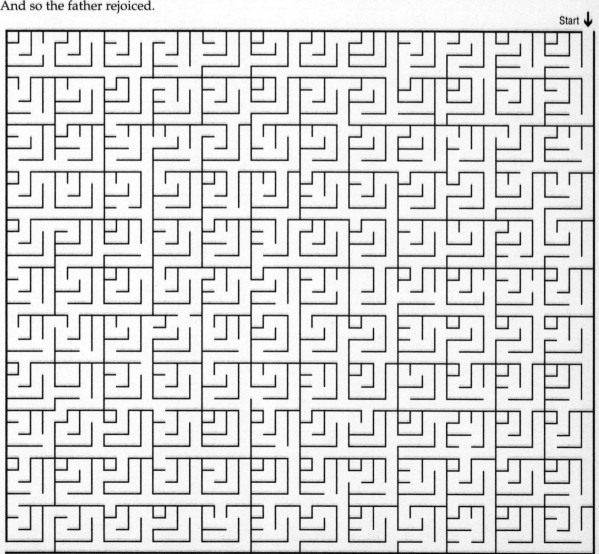

End ←

*S*ome fatherly advice goes a long way.

Clue: MESSIAH *is* BROOJZL

B C   D J M M D R   V L J D T Q R Y'

M L R O R   M L J Y N O   J

G Q J M R   M W   C W K'   O W   M L Z M

C W K   B Z C   Y W M   O J Y.   Z Y T

J P   Z Y C W Y R   O J Y O'   G R

L Z I R   Z Y   Z T I W V Z M R

G J M L   M L R   P Z M L R Q'   H R O K O

V L Q J O M   M L R   Q J N L M R W K O.

Z Y T   L R   L J B O R D P   J O   M L R

U Q W U J M J Z M J W Y   P W Q   W K Q

O J Y O'   Z Y T   Y W M   P W Q

W K Q O   W Y D C   X K M   Z D O W

P W Q   M L R   G L W D R   G W Q D T.

Ruth and Boaz

*I*n addition to being a beautiful love story, the book of Ruth is an example of the fact that love will find a way to communicate even when communication is difficult. Ruth, a young widow, elected to leave the land of her birth to accompany her much-loved mother-in-law Naomi to the land of Naomi's birth. In doing this, Ruth committed herself to help support Naomi in a land where Ruth knew no one and, perhaps, did not even speak the language.

But God honored Ruth's loyalty to Naomi. While gathering grain left by the reapers in Boaz's fields, Ruth caught his eye. From that time until the day they married, Boaz and Ruth communicated their love and respect for one another in some unique ways that you might enjoy reading about in this Old Testament book.

This maze has two starting points, but they both end up in the same place. Help Ruth and Boaz "tell" one another what is in their hearts.

*A*s you complete the words to one of the most famous Christmas carols in the world—"O Come, All Ye Faithful"—you'll have the clues you need to complete this crossword grid.

Stanza #1:

O come, _____ ye _____ , _____ and _____ , O come _____ , O come ye _____ _____ ; Come _____
4 Down   18 Down   31 Across   21 Across   61 Across   39 Across 6 Down   35 Down

_____ him, born the _____ of _____ ;
71 Across   52 Down   63 Across

Refrain:

O come, let _____ adore him, O _____ , let us _____ him, O come, _____ us adore _____ , _____
32 Across   7 Down   16 Down   38 Across   46 Across 12 Down

_____ Lord.
34 Down

Stanza #2:

God of God, Light of _____ , _____ ! _____ _____ not the _____ womb; Very God, _____ , not
9 Across   60 Down 23 Across 45 Down   54 Across   26 Across

_____ ;
56 Down

Stanza #3:

Sing, _____ of angels, _____ _____ _____ , _____ , _____ ye _____ of heav'n _____ ; Glory to
14 Across   41 Down 67 Down 44 Across 72 Across 27 Across 43 Down   8 Across

_____ , in the _____ ;
51 Across   13 Down

Stanza #4:

_____ how the _____ , _____ to _____ _____ , Leaving their _____ , draw _____ to _____ ; _____ too
47 Across   3 Down   30 Down 19 Across 24 Down   2 Down   17 Across 33 Down 25 Across

_____ thither, _____ _____ joyful _____ ;
25 Down   53 Down 42 Down   40 Down

Stanza #5:

_____ , for us _____ , _____ and _____ the _____ , We would _____ thee, with _____ and _____ ;
29 Across   69 Across 22 Down 20 Down   15 Across   5 Across   64 Down   49 Across

Who would _____ love _____ , _____ us _____ _____ ?
          70 Down   66 Across 28 Down 3 Across 48 Down

Stanza #6:

_____ , _____ , _____ _____ thee, Born _____ happy _____ ; _____ , to thee _____ all _____
36 Across 65 Down 1 Down 33 Across   21 Down   37 Across 62 Down   11 Across   59 Across

_____ ; _____ _____ the _____ , _____ in 40 Across 55 Across ;
10 Down 50 Down 57 Across 58 Down 68 Across

Word Pool

ABHORS ABOVE ADORE ALL AND ANGELS APPEARING AWE BE BEGOTTEN
BEHOLD BEND BETHLEHEM CHILD CHOIRS CHRIST CITIZENS COME CRADLE
CREATED DEARLY EMBRACE EXULTATION FAITHFUL FATHER FLESH FLOCKS
FOOTSTEPS GAZE GIV'N GLORY GOD GREET HE HIGHEST HIM HIS IN JESUS
JOYFUL KING LET LIGHT LO LORD LOVE LOVING MANGER MORNING NIGH
NOT NOW OF OUR POOR SEE SHEPHERDS SING SINNERS SO SUMMONED
THE THEE THIS TO TRIUMPHANT US VIRGIN'S WE WILL WORD YE YEA
(NOTE: A few words are used more than once.)

*W*as Jesus the first to say, "actions speak louder than words"?

Clue: MESSIAH *is* RPIIEOU

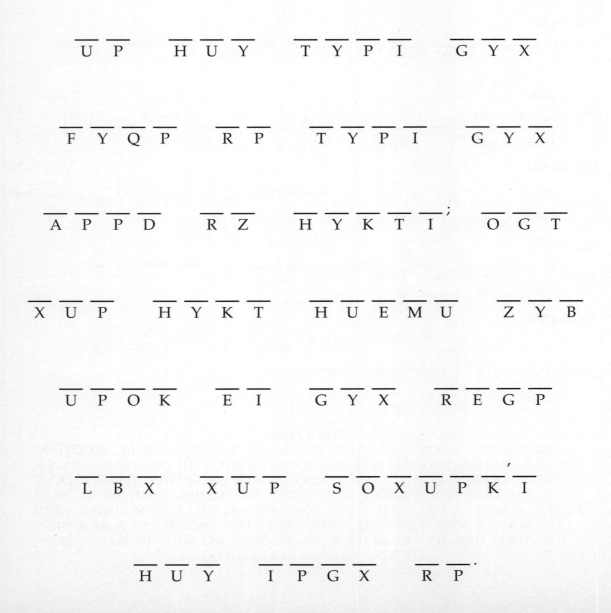

U P   H U Y   T Y P I   G Y X

F Y Q P   R P   T Y P I   G Y X

A P P D   R Z   H Y K T I ;   O G T

X U P   H Y K T   H U E M U   Z Y B

U P O K   E I   G Y X   R E G P

L B X   X U P   S O X U P K I '

H U Y   I P G X   R P .

Up to Jerusalem

*I*n New Testament times, the Jews celebrated Passover in Jerusalem. Who among them could forget the long-ago enslavement of God's people by Pharaoh . . . the plagues that befell the Egyptians as Pharaoh ignored Moses' entreaties . . . and finally, the most devastating plague of all: death of the firstborn child and animal in every Egyptian household?

But the children of Israel were spared. Following Moses' orders, they ate the first Passover meal, put the blood of the lamb on their doorposts, and avoided the fate of their earthly masters. And Pharaoh let God's people go.

Beginning on the bottom line, connect a string of letters that form a three-word phrase telling us what Passover symbolizes.

↙ End

S	A	L	J	E	R	U	S	A	L	E	M	J	E	R	U	S	E	A	L	E	M	J	E	R
J	E	R	U	S	J	E	R	U	S	A	L	E	M	S	A	G	L	E	M	J	E	R	U	S
S	A	L	E	J	E	R	U	J	E	R	U	S	R	U	A	S	A	L	E	M	J	E	R	U
J	E	R	J	E	R	U	S	A	L	E	J	E	R	D	U	S	J	E	R	U	S	A	L	E
L	E	M	S	A	J	E	R	U	S	A	L	E	E	R	N	U	S	A	L	E	M	J	E	R
R	U	S	A	L	E	M	J	E	J	E	R	U	S	J	E	O	R	U	S	A	L	E	M	U
S	A	L	J	E	R	U	S	A	L	E	J	E	R	M	B	J	E	R	U	S	A	L	J	E
M	J	E	R	U	S	J	E	R	U	S	U	S	O	A	L	E	M	J	E	R	U	S	A	L
A	L	J	E	R	U	S	J	E	R	U	F	R	S	A	L	E	M	U	S	A	L	E	M	J
J	E	R	U	J	S	A	L	J	U	E	J	E	R	U	S	A	L	E	M	J	E	R	U	S
A	L	E	M	J	E	J	E	R	C	U	S	J	E	R	U	S	A	L	J	E	R	S	A	L
M	J	E	J	E	R	U	S	A	J	N	E	R	U	S	J	E	R	U	S	A	L	J	E	R
A	J	E	R	U	S	J	E	R	A	U	S	A	L	J	E	R	U	S	J	E	R	U	S	A
J	E	R	U	J	E	R	U	R	S	A	L	E	R	U	S	A	L	E	M	E	M	J	E	R
L	E	M	J	E	J	E	R	U	E	S	A	J	E	R	U	S	A	L	E	M	S	A	L	E
S	J	E	R	U	S	A	J	V	J	E	R	U	A	L	E	M	R	J	E	R	U	S	A	L
A	L	E	J	E	R	U	I	A	L	E	S	A	L	E	M	J	E	R	U	S	A	L	E	M
M	J	E	R	U	J	L	E	R	U	S	A	L	E	M	E	R	U	S	A	L	E	M	J	E
S	A	J	E	R	U	S	E	A	L	E	M	J	E	R	U	S	A	L	E	M	J	E	R	U
J	E	R	U	S	A	D	J	E	M	A	L	E	M	J	E	R	U	S	A	L	E	M	J	E

Start ↗

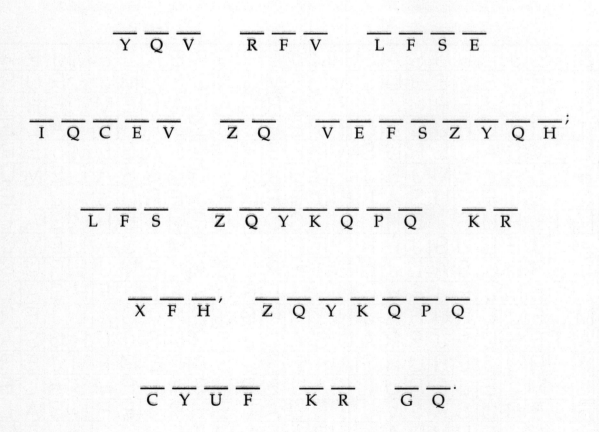

These words have been a constant source of comfort and reassurance to Christians since the moment Christ spoke them.

Clue: MESSIAH *is* GQUUKCI

— — —   — — —   — — — —
Y Q V   R F V   L F S E

— — — — —   — —   — — — — — — — —;
I Q C E V   Z Q   V E F S Z Y Q H

— — —   — — — — — — —   — —
L F S   Z Q Y K Q P Q   K R

— — —'   — — — — — — —
X F H   Z Q Y K Q P Q

— — — —   — —   — —.
C Y U F   K R   G Q

Next to the name of each of these Bible figures is the jumbled name of his mother. Write the mothers' names in the blanks of the grid, and you'll discover a message each of these sons could have given to his mother. (A Scripture reference is provided if you need it.)

1.	SOLOMON	B H T A E B H S A	(1 Kings l:15–17)
2.	JOSEPH	L A C E R H	(Genesis 35:24)
3.	GERSHOM	Z I O A P R H P	(Exodus 2:21–22)
4.	GAD	H I A Z L P	(Genesis 30:9–11)
5.	JESUS	R A Y M	(Luke 2:4–7, 21)
6.	REUEL	B A M T S E A H	(Genesis 36:10)
7.	MOSES	E C B O H J E D	(Exodus 6:20)
8.	OBED	U T R H	(Ruth 4:13, 17)
9.	REUBEN	E H L A	(Genesis 29:32)
10.	CAIN	V E E	(Genesis 4:1)
11.	ISHMAEL	G A R A H	(Genesis 16:15)
12.	ISAAC	H A S R A	(Genesis 21:2–3)
13.	ELIPHAZ	D H A A	(Genesis 36:10)
14.	SAMUEL	A N H N H A	(1 Samuel 1:20)
15.	JOHN MARK	A Y R M	(Acts 12:12)

1   — — — — — — — —

2   — — — — — —

3   — — — — — — —

4   — — — — — —

5   — — — —

6   — — — — — — —

7   — — — — — — —

8   — — — —

9   — — — —

10   — — —

11   — — — — — —

12   — — — — —

13   — — — —

14   — — — — — —

15   — — —

*H*ave you ever had a perfect day? Isn't it nice to know that eternity is going to be just one perfect day after another, after another . . .

Bonus:

Unscramble the circled letters to reveal our "perfect home."

___ ___ ___ ___ ___ ___

Across

4 The perfect "statute" of the Lord converts the soul (Psalm 19:7)

7 When the perfect comes, the "portion" will be done away with (1 Corinthians 13:10)

8 No "untruth" was found in Jesus' mouth (1 Peter 2:22)

10 Be perfect as your _____ in heaven is perfect (Matthew 5:48)

11 This apostle wasn't perfected, but he pressed on (Philippians 3:1, 12)

13 Preposition

14 The faithful didn't receive the "pledge" and won't be made perfect apart from us (Hebrews 11:39–40)

16 Regarding (abbr.)

17 After we've "endured pain" a while, God will perfect us (1 Peter 5:10)

19 "Let _____ have its perfect work, that you may be perfect . . ." (James 1:4)

21 A peace offering could have no "fault" (Leviticus 22:21)

23 This bondservant of Christ prayed that the Colossians would stand perfect in God's will (Colossians 4:12)

27 If we say we have no sin, the _____ is not in us (1 John 1:8)

28 Abraham's faith, combined with his "actions," perfected his faith (James 2:21–22)

29 Christ was a Lamb without _____ or spot (1 Peter 1:19)

30 God told Abram, "Walk before Me and be 'without culpability'" (Genesis 17:1)

35 The perfect Son became the "writer" of eternal salvation (Hebrews 5:9)

36 Scripture was given to make us "whole" (2 Timothy 3:16–17)

37 Perfect love casts out _____ (1 John 4:18)

Down

1 The "commander" of our salvation was made perfect through sufferings (Hebrews 2:10)

2 After the "exam," Job would come forth as gold (Job 23:10)

3 David's wasn't broken; it would be perfect, he told God in Psalm 101:2

5 Not B.C., but _____

6 We're glad you're strong when we're _____ , Paul told the Corinthians, that they may be made complete (2 Corinthians 13:9)

7 God keeps us in perfect _____ when our minds are stayed on Him (Isaiah 26:3)

9 The king of _____ (not Sidon) was the seal of perfection (Ezekiel 28:12)

10 Cleansing all filthiness of the _____ and spirit would perfect holiness in the Corinthians (2 Corinthians 7:1)

11 Not A.M., but _____

12 You and me

14 "Out of the mouth of babes . . . you have perfected _____ " (Matthew 21:16)

15 Everyone who is perfectly trained will be like his "instructor" (Luke 6:40)

18 "He is the 'Refuge,' His work is perfect" (Deuteronomy 32:4)

20 A just man, perfect in his generations (Genesis 6:9)

22 Paul wanted to perfect what the Thessalonians' "trust" lacked (1 Thessalonians 3:9–10)

24 Our High Priest is "hallowed" (Hebrews 7:26)

25 Was the flesh making the Galatians perfect, and not the _____ ? (Galatians 3:3)

26 God's _____ is made perfect in weakness (2 Corinthians 12:9)

28 "Prove what is that good and acceptable and perfect _____ of God" (Romans 12:2)

31 "Charity" is the bond of perfection, says Paul (Colossians 3:14)

32 Jesus was tempted as we are, but was without "transgression" (Hebrews 4:15)

33 God made David's "path" perfect (Psalm 18:32)

34 To be perfect, Jesus told the rich man, sell your possessions and give to the _____ (Matthew 19:21)

CROWN OF LIFE

*I*n Revelation 2:10, the angel to the church of Smyrna spoke these words of the Lord, "Do not fear any of those things which you are about to suffer. Indeed, the devil is about to throw some of you into prison, that you may be tested, and you will have tribulation ten days. Be faithful until death, and I will give you the crown of life."

Crowns have always been symbols of royalty. The cross is frequently combined with the crown to create a church symbol. It represents the reward of everlasting life given to those who accept the sacrifice of Jesus and believe in Him as their Savior.

Start →

← End

*W*hat is God like? Find twenty attributes of God in the letter box below.

```
P   X   L   T   F   R   T   N   E   I   T   A   P
S   O   G   R   A   C   I   O   U   S   N   T   L
L   I   O   R   I   A   S   E   J   O   E   N   O
U   R   O   E   T   E   R   N   A   L   T   S   V
F   A   D   U   H   H   R   R   X   G   O   P   T
I   W   L   A   F   C   G   O   R   E   P   V   N
C   O   U   B   U   R   O   I   L   W   I   S   E
R   D   O   Y   L   O   H   X   L   T   N   P   I
E   T   A   N   O   I   S   S   A   P   M   O   C
M   R   O   S   T   N   W   I   C   X   O   R   S
J   U   S   T   E   L   B   A   T   U   M   M   I
S   E   T   R   I   G   H   T   E   O   U   S   N
B   N   G   I   E   R   E   V   O   S   H   S   M
U   L   T   N   E   S   E   R   P   I   N   M   O
```

Word Pool

COMPASSIONATE ETERNAL FAITHFUL GOOD GRACIOUS HOLY
IMMUTABLE JUST LIGHT LOVE MERCIFUL OMNIPOTENT
OMNIPRESENT OMNISCIENT ONE PATIENT RIGHTEOUS
SOVEREIGN TRUE WISE

*M*any clues relate to the Sabbath.

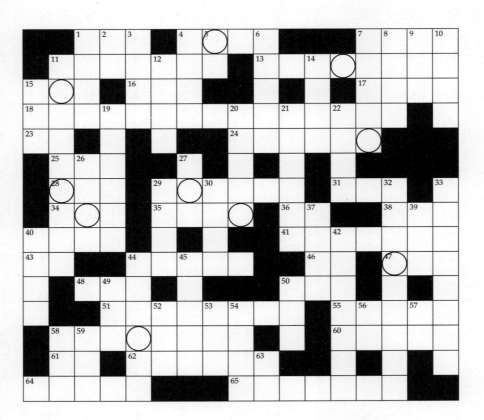

Unscramble the circled letters
to reveal a phrase related to the Sabbath.

___ __ __ __ __ __ __   __ __ __

Across

1 High school organization for tomorrow's teachers (abbr.)
2 Mercy _____ (part of the ark of the covenant) (Leviticus 16:2)
7 Roman garb
11 The disciples did this to heads of grain on the Sabbath (Matthew 12:1)
13 Deliriously happy
15 Sound of discovery
16 Masculine, objective case
17 Quote
18 A man was stoned for doing this on the Sabbath (2 words) (Numbers 15:32–36)
23 Initials of a television evangelist
24 Truly, indeed
25 "_____ _____ little teapot, short and stout . . ."
28 Pedro's sun
29 Stitching
31 Affirmative
34 First lady
35 Home for #34 Across
36 Single word title for popular song about Him
38 King James English for #31 Across
40 Its yield depends on the soil it's in
41 Instructor
43 "Love one another; _____ I have loved you" (John 13:34)
44 Jesus did this as He taught in the temple (John 8:20)
46 "Gimme that _____' time religion"
47 Pie _____ mode
48 "Did _____ not know that I must be about My Father's business?" (Luke 2:49)
50 A king of Judah; Jehoshaphat's father (1 Kings 22:41)
51 Not refuted
55 Grill in the oven
58 Yard worker
60 Quarrel
61 Between la and do
62 Reply
64 Remorseful
65 Proclaim

Down

1 Horizontal
2 You, to Caesar
3 Pain
4 Prefix for half
5 Nickname for Queen Elizabeth's youngest son
6 Razz
7 Garish
8 Name in an elevator
9 "_____ along, lil' dogie"
10 Passes with flying colors (as a test)
11 Jesus' Sabbath critics (Luke 14:1)
12 Captain of the *Enterprise*
14 A "good" place for seed
15 Long time _____
19 Jesus did this for the man with a withered hand on the Sabbath (Luke 6:6–10)
20 Jesus' disciples were criticized for rubbing this between their hands on the Sabbath (Luke 6:1)
21 Jesus did this in the synagogue on the Sabbath (Mark 1:21)
22 Jesus healed a man's eyes with this on the Sabbath (John 9:14)
26 Relocate
27 Sabbath command: "Take up your _____ and walk" (John 5:11)
29 Ooze
30 The Sabbath is the seventh day of this
32 Apostles' Sabbath location (Acts 13:42)
33 Jesus spoke in these on the Sabbath (Luke 14:7)
37 One kind of love
39 Electric fish
40 Foolish place to build a house (Matthew 7:26)
42 Mississippi neighbor
44 Christian "Sabbath"
45 Baking places
49 "_____ Father in heaven, hallowed be . . ."
50 Tally
52 Daniel shared the lions'
53 Modern
54 Angered
56 Sign at a crossing
57 A, e, _____ , o, _____
58 Popular Ford model of 60s song
59 Atmosphere
63 Between do and mi

*U*nscramble the names of these twenty-three people mentioned in the New Testament, and discover in the process what they had in common. (Check the Scripture
Pool for help.)

SISLA   — — — — —

RAKM   — — — —

ITHOMTY   — — — — — — —

ARNYNTSU   — — — — — — — —

AGBUAS   — — — — — —

UHTUCEYS   — — — — — — — —

YTHICSCU   — — — — — — — —

ANEASE   — — — — — —

KUEL   — — — —

ASGIU   — — — — —

MIARDAS   — — — — — — —

DAYLI   — — — — —

RMYA   — — — —

ISRPICLAL   — — — — — — — —

ORPTUHSIM   — — — — — — — — —

RASETUS   — — — — — — —

QIAAUL   — — — — — —

ARIRASUTCSH   — — — — — — — — — — —

TIAHBTA   — — — — — — —

ASVISLNU   — — — — — — — —

OSAPRTE   — — — — — — —

LIOCNREUS   — — — — — — — — —

EINOSUMS   — — — — — — — —

Scripture Pool

ACTS 9:33, 36; 10:1; 11:28; 12:12; 16:14, 25; 17:34; 18:18; 19:9, 22, 29; 20:4, 9
COLOSSIANS 4:9, 14   1 THESSALONIANS 1:1

*I*n John 14:6, Jesus gives us instruction as to how we are able to approach God. To reveal Jesus' words, begin with the circled letter and trace from letter to letter, until you have spelled out each word of the scripture. You may move in any direction, but only move to adjacent squares. Do not use any letter twice. When you finish, you will have used every letter in the puzzle. The first two moves are done for you.

N	E	F	I	L	W	A
O	O	N	E	H	E	Y
C	E	H	(I)	T	M	T
M	O	T	D	A	T	H
S	E	N	A	U	R	E
T	O	T	H	T	O	R
T	H	A	G	U	T	H
H	F	E	H	C	E	T
E	R	E	X	M	E	P

OVERFLOWING CUP

*I*n Psalm 23:5, David joyfully exclaims, "My cup runs over." The cup pictured in the maze is a communion cup bearing two important Christian symbols. The first, the fish, is widely used to represent the same thing that it did to the early Christians who used it as a secret symbol to identify themselves to one another as followers of Christ at a time when open confession of one's faith was dangerous.

The second symbol, the letters IHS, is frequently used on sacred objects among Christian churches of all denominations. Often misinterpreted to mean "in His service," the letters are actually the first three letters of Jesus' name spelled IHSOUS in Greek.

*H*idden in the letter box below are names of sixteen false gods and idols mentioned in the Bible. Circle each one as you find it. After you have found the names, read the remaining letters left to right to find out what the apostle Paul wrote to the church at Corinth about false gods.

```
F  L  E  E  F  R  A  O  M  I  D  O  L  A  T
R  Y  I  D  N  O  N  N  O  M  T  W  A  N  T
Y  O  U  T  I  O  A  H  M  O  L  E  C  H  A
V  E  D  F  S  E  M  L  L  C  O  W  S  H  I
P  W  A  D  R  A  M  M  E  L  E  C  H  I  T
H  D  G  E  O  M  E  O  N  I  S  Y  O  U  C
A  N  O  N  C  O  L  T  D  M  R  I  L  N  K
T  H  N  E  H  T  E  R  O  T  H  S  A  C  L
U  P  O  T  F  T  C  H  E  L  O  R  A  E  D
A  N  D  A  T  N  H  H  E  C  U  S  B  P  O
F  D  E  M  O  B  E  E  L  Z  E  B  U  B  M
O  N  S  M  Y  O  M  U  C  M  A  N  N  O  T
P  A  M  U  R  T  O  A  R  K  E  O  F  T  H
E  I  L  Z  E  U  S  E  O  R  O  B  E  N  D
R  S  T  A  B  L  H  E  A  N  D  O  F  T  H
E  T  A  B  L  E  O  F  D  E  M  O  N  S  ⤙
```

Word Pool
ADRAMMELECH ANAMMELECH ASHTORETH BAAL BEELZEBUB BEL
CHEMOSH DAGON HERMES MILCOM MOLECH NEBO NISROCH
RIMMON TAMMUZ ZEUS

31

*A*ll chapter and verse references in these clues are from 2 Kings, unless stated otherwise. Many of the clues have to do with Elisha and his prophetic mission.

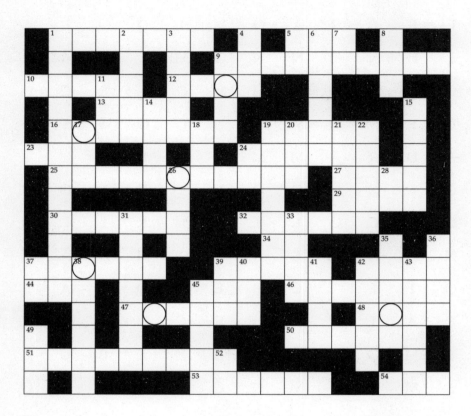

Bonus:

Unscramble the circled letters to reveal
the name of the prophet who anointed Elisha.

_____ _____ _____ _____ _____ _____

Across

1 City of famine rescued by four lepers (7:1, 3)
5 Peaches _____ cream
9 _____ woman—for whom Elisha prophesied a son (4:12)
10 What the diners claimed was in the stew pot (4:40)
12 Region
13 Finest
16 Wall coverings or old-fashioned ointment bandages
19 What Elisha had placed on the dead child's face (4:29)
23 Lincoln's nickname
24 Fashion designer of note
25 Where Naaman was told to dip (2 words) (5:10)
27 Prominent facial feature
29 Adorable
30 Elisha's mentor (1 Kings 19:19–21)
32 Collar or necklace
34 Its head floated (6:5–6)
37 Elisha's servant (4:25)
39 Where the ax went (6:5)
42 Sunday song
44 Mining product
45 _____-Hadad; suicidal king of Syria (8:7–15)
46 Organic
47 Elisha was given twenty loaves of _____ bread with which he fed one hundred people (4:42–44)
48 Wee
50 Rouge kitty (2 words)
51 How Elijah left (2:11)
53 City surrounded by chariots of fire (6:13–17)
54 Elisha prayed, "LORD, open the eyes of these _____ , that they may see" (6:20)

Down

1 Mutton/lamb producer
2 Evidence of fire
3 Angry
4 Mortgage loan type
5 Article for word beginning with a vowel
6 Jordan bather (5:9–10)
7 Initials for a decimeter
8 Widow's supply of this was stretched to fill all the jars (4:2)
11 Schedule entry for times not yet determined
14 Recipe direction
15 Number of days they searched for Elijah after his ascent (2:17)
17 Hawaiian greeting token
18 _____ de Janeiro
19 Elisha's father (1 Kings 19:19)
20 Sun's action on skin
21 Yard divider
22 Elisha's cure for the poisonous stew (4:40–41)
24 Cassette tape's successor
26 Cousin of Jesus
28 Ave.
31 From queen to dog food—Elisha's prophecy came true for her (9:36–37)
33 Elisha was behind twelve yoke of these when Elijah commissioned him (1 Kings 19:19)
35 A country at war with Israel (6:8)
36 Solely
37 "_____ into all the world and preach the gospel" (Mark 16:15)
38 Abdominal rupture
39 Tiny
40 One or another
41 Fury
42 Boxlike pen for rabbits
43 Elisha inherited Elijah's (2:13)
45 Insipid
49 Number of widow's sons (4:1)
52 "_____ good to those who hate you" (Matthew 5:44)

*S*tring together the letters below to reveal one of the Bible's most famous verses about love.

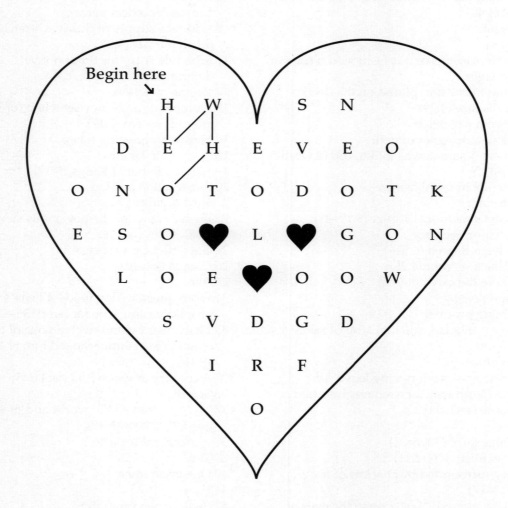

Rahab's Escape Route

When Joshua sent spies into the city of Jericho, they were aided in their escape by a woman named Rahab. Rahab was a prostitute, but she had heard about the power of the true God of the Israelites. She believed that Jericho, though surrounded by a high wall, would be conquered by Israel. She offered to help the spies in exchange for safety for her and her family when the Israelites invaded Jericho.

Rahab's house was actually on the wall. After hiding the spies on the roof while her house was searched, she let them down the side of the wall by a rope and they made good their escape in the darkness. When the walls of Jericho fell, Rahab and her family were the only ones left alive.

Beginning at Rahab's window, travel only on stones that are touching. Exit anywhere on the ground as long as the last stone touches the ground.

After leaving Egypt, the Israelites needed the discipline of a godly life. So God gave them specific rules to follow to help them stay on track. This puzzle is based on the book of Deuteronomy.

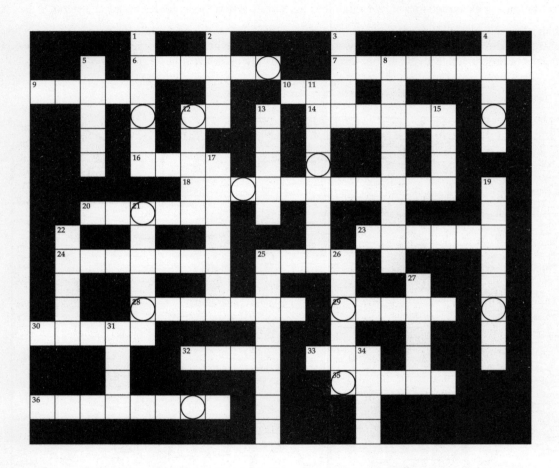

Bonus:

Unscramble the circled letters to reveal the place
where the Israelites were about to enter when
the message of Deuteronomy was given to them.

___ ___ ___ ___ ___ ___ ___   ___ ___ ___ ___

Across

6 Don't take God's name this way (2 words) (5:11)

7 And "don't forget" the Lord your God (8:18)

9 First month (pl.) in Hebrew year; observe it! (16:1)

10 Comes in cubes

12 Part-time (abbr.)

14 A fellow "Israelite" slave earned freedom after six years (15:12)

16 The people could slaughter and eat this within their gates (12:15)

18 An "idol" was forbidden (2 words) (5:8)

20 Their duty was to hear cases (1:16)

23 Don't forsake the "priest" within your gates (14:27)

24 "Adhere to" the commandments (12:32)

25 Sea creatures with _____ and scales could be eaten (14:9)

28 A perfect and just weight and _____ was a must (25:15)

29 "You . . . shall take 'pledges' in His name" (6:13)

30 The required Feast of _____ celebrated firstfruits (16:10)

32 You shall have none other before Him (5:7)

33 Affirmative response

35 At Passover, the sacred assembly met on day _____ (16:8)

36 The third-generation Edomite and _____ could enter the Lord's assembly (23:7–8)

Down

1 Following God's statutes was the Israelites' "knowledge" and understanding (4:6)

2 "Throw" out all your enemies, God commanded (6:19)

3 Don't plant one as a wooden image near the altar you build (16:21)

4 A release of debts was granted every _____ years (15:1)

5 Take your "one-tenth" (sing.) to the place God chooses (12:6)

8 Enter no "wedlocks" with your enemies (7:3)

11 Teach your "offspring" what God has done (4:9)

12 Suggest _____ before you make war (20:10–12)

13 Remember that you were a "bondservant" in Egypt (15:15)

15 When a man took a new _____ , he was excused from war and business for one year (24:5)

17 Sew these on the four corners of your clothing (22:12)

19 Obeying the commandments meant a "benefit" (11:27)

21 Beware a dreamer of _____ ; God uses him to test you (13:1–3)

22 The commandments should be written on the doorposts of this dwelling (6:9)

25 Circumcise this "covering" of your heart, Moses said (10:16)

26 If someone close to you encourages you to worship false gods, throw these at him until he dies (13:10)

27 Don't do a close one to the front of your head for the dead (14:1)

31 "Hang onto" the commandments (4:2)

34 Don't forget, children of Israel, what your eyes have _____ God do (4:9)

All adult Jewish males were required to go "up to Jerusalem" for the three major feasts of the year: the Feast of Passover, the Feast of Weeks, and the Feast of Tabernacles. Help the sojourners below get to Jerusalem in record time.

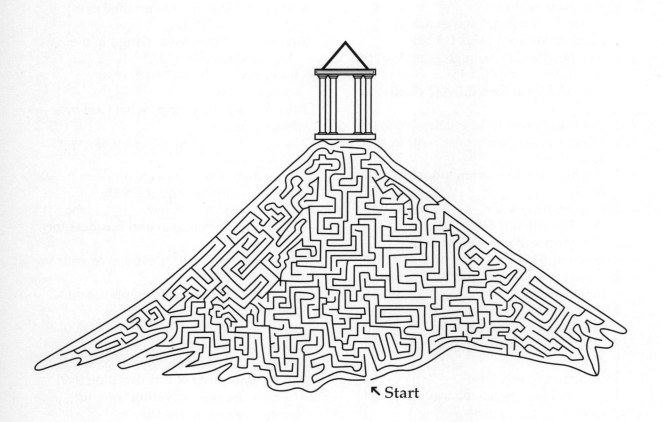

↖ Start

Galatians 5:19–21 lists seventeen specific "works of the flesh" that are contrary to the work of the Holy Spirit in a person's life. Paul warns that "those who practice such things will not inherit the kingdom of God." See how many of these fleshly sins you can find in the letter box below before consulting the Scriptures.
(Note: Two of the "works" have more than one word.)

```
L C N T U S N O I T N E T N O C I E E
E L E R N S Y M O I S R S S M R B W A
N N A E O E R F U N S O O U T M C D B
V E R C T N M O U R E R R N K E N E U
E S E I A N U R D C D D U C S S E N R
R S V O L E L N E I D R I E H A H S
E H E N O K E I S R F I S H A R D T T
H O L S D N W C S A O D Y S E E Y A S
E D R I A U D A H T R E R V R Y V R S
W U I T Y R E T L U D A T T N D N W E
U T E S R D F I B F N N A R I E E F C
B B S J S W O O U L I H L S W I S O L
T U R S T E S N R E C N O T E N N S F
U O S L E A N T S S A S D V Y T O T H
E E S E L F I S H A M B I T I O N S E
R S I W L O E U I O T O S O D I S R R
I D E D M I W S I O I S N W B T E U L
S Y N N S E D S R S N S T A M S E B S
I V L E L U O L A E J S H S I E S T W
D S R S S I D S S E N N A E L C N U D
S E E S N J E A L O U S I E S T N O C
H N N A I O N S S E M U R U N C O L E
```

You may find the *WAY* to work this puzzle in the *TRAIL* of scriptures given . . . all of which trace a *PATH* to a better life.

Across

1 A military address
4 On's opposite
6 Initials of *The Lion, the Witch, and the Wardrobe* author
10 Illustration
12 "_____ for yourselves this day whom you will serve" (Joshua 24:15)
14 British slang for "thanks!"
15 Decipher
16 Small collie-like dog
17 "These men are the _____(s) of the Most High God, who #38 Across to us the way of #24 Down" (Acts 16:17)
19 "_____ is a way that #9 Down to a man" (Proverbs 14:12)
20 Comes between K and N
21 Despised
22 Wise men went another way to avoid seeing him (Matthew 2:12)
24 International signal of distress
25 Earthy red or yellow color (British spelling)
26 What Miss Muffet was eating with #27 Across
27 See #26 Across
28 Large Hawaiian thistle flower
29 Hawaiian welcome token
30 Maine's southern neighbor (abbr.)
32 Regarding flight (combined form)
35 Crush
38 See #17 Across
40 Early religious song form
41 What your bread is doing in the morning
43 Destination for Paul and Sopater (Acts 20:4)
44 Paul's home for three months until he fled the Jews who plotted against him (Acts 20:2)
45 The losers: "_____-rans"
46 Charley-horse
47 Pilfer
48 "_____ stands in the path of sinners" (Psalm 1:1)

Down

1 What Elisha caused to float
2 Procession
3 Sign
4 "The _____ Rugged Cross"
5 Symbol for iron
6 Sonny's "ex"
7 Favored filet fish
8 He found a way out of Sodom and Gomorrah
9 See #19 Across (2 words)
10 Terra cotta container (2 words)
11 "#14 Down me Your way, O LORD, and lead me in a smooth _____" (Psalm 27:11)
12 A yellow cheese
13 Farm structure
14 See #11 Down
16 Beach
17 "And yet I _____ you a more excellent way" (1 Corinthians 12:31)
18 Extremely

19 "I am the way, the _____, and the life" (John 14:6)
23 Science of commerce and exchange
24 See #17 Across
28 "But without faith it is impossible to _____ Him" (Hebrews 11:6)
31 Unlocks
32 Buzzer
33 Ritual
34 Droop
35 Petite
36 Tree's northern covering
37 Paul's frequent "escape route"
39 Parts of an interlocking wheel
42 An object made of mesh
45 Confidential rehab group for persons with a drinking addiction (abbr.)

THE NESTORIAN CROSS

*T*his cross design was used by Christians as early as A.D. 44. It was not called the Nestorian Cross, however, for four more centuries.

Nestorius was a monk who became presbyter at Antioch, and eventually, the Patriarch of Constantinople in A.D. 428. He became involved in a dispute between the Alexandrian and Antiochian schools of thought in what became known as the "Christological Controversy," and as a result, he was deposed at the Council of Ephesus in A.D. 431. He spent four years in Antioch, then was banished to upper Egypt, where he suffered great indignities before his death in A.D. 451.

His loyal followers, known as Nestorians, continued to preach the gospel in Persia and eventually took the message of Christ east to India and China. They carried with them this cross shape, and thus it became known as the Nestorian Cross. Historians believe it is the first cross ever taken to China, and several ancient examples of it are still found there.

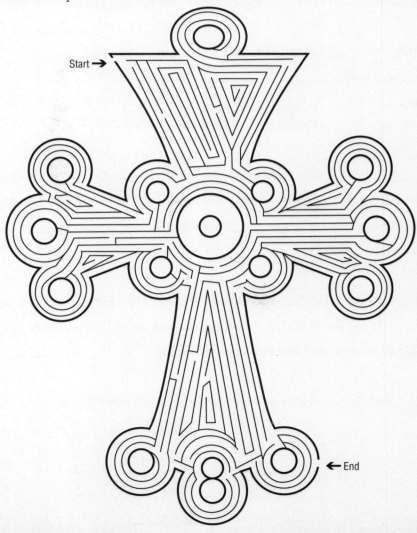

Start →

← End

39

Put the missing words from 1 Corinthians 13 in the acrostic grid on the next page . . . and you'll complete an important message about the theme of this chapter. (Note: The first part of the message has been provided for you.)

Though I speak with the tongues of men and of angels, but have not love, I have become sounding brass or a clanging cymbal. And though I have the gift of prophecy, and understand all mysteries and all knowledge, and though I have all faith, so that I could remove mountains, but have not love, I am nothing. And though I bestow all my goods to feed the poor, and though I give my body to be burned, but have not love, it profits me nothing.

Love _____ long and _____ _____ ; love does _____ _____ ; love does _____ _____ _____ , is
     17   15   5   1

_____ _____ _____ ; does _____ _____ _____ , does _____ _____ _____ _____ , is _____ _____ ,
    4   12   13   10

_____ _____ ; does _____ _____ _____ , but rejoices in the _____ ; _____ all
    9   6   18   22

things, _____ all things, _____ all things, _____ all things.
    8   16   3

Love _____ _____ . But whether there are prophecies, they will fail; whether there are tongues,
    19

they will cease; whether there is knowledge, it will vanish away. For we know in part and we

prophesy in part. But when that which is _____ has come, then that which is in part will be done
    20

away.

When I was a child, I spoke as a child, I understood as a child, I thought as a child; but when I

_____ _____ _____ , I put away childish things. For now we see in a mirror, dimly, but then _____
    11

_____ _____ . Now I know in part, but then I shall know just _____ _____ _____ _____ _____ .
    14   21

And now _____ faith, hope, love, these three; but the _____ of these is love.
    2   7

1   _ _ _ **P** _ _ _ _ _ _ _ _ _ _

2   _ _ _ _ **E**

3   _ _ _ _ **R** _ _

4   _ _ _ _ _ **F** _ _ _ _

5   _ _ _ **E** _ _ _

6   _ _ _ _ _ _ _ _ **C** _ _ _ _ _ _ _ _ _

7   _ _ _ **T** _ _ _

8   _ _ **L** _ _ _ _

9   _ _ _ _ _ _ **O** _ _ _ _

10   _ _ _ _ _ _ **V** _ _ _ _

THERE IS NO FEAR IN LOVE, BUT . . .

11   _ _ **C** _ _ _ _ _

12   _ _ _ _ _ **A** _ _ _ _ _ _

13   _ _ _ **S** _ _ _ _ _ _ _

14   _ _ _ _ **T** _ _ _ _

15   _ **S** _ _ _ _

16   _ **O** _ _ _

17   _ **U** _ _ _ _

18   **T** _ _ _ _

19   _ _ _ _ **F** _ _ _ _

20   _ **E** _ _ _ _

21   _ _ _ **A** _ _ _ _ _ _ _ _

22   _ _ _ **R** _

*K*ing Solomon reigned over all Israel—but not without the help of officials and governors. Below is an organizational chart of Solomon's administrators as they are named in 1 Kings 4:1–19. Administrators, of course, must interact with one another in order for a kingdom to function smoothly. Your goal is to place these names (not titles) in the crossword grid . . . we've given you a few letters as a start.

KING
Solomon

OFFICIALS

Azariah
Priest

Elihoreph and Ahijah
Scribes

Jehoshaphat
Recorder

Zadok and Abiathar
Priests

Zabud
Priest and Friend

OFFICERS

Benaiah
Army

Azariah
Officers

Ahishar
Household

Adoniram
Labor Force

GOVERNORS

Ben-Hur
Mountains of Ephraim

Ben-Deker
Makaz, Shaalbim, Beth Shemesh, Elon Beth Hanan

Ben-Hesed
Arubboth

Ben-Abinadab
Dor

Baana
Taanach, Megiddo, Beth Shean

Ben-Geber
Ramoth Gilead

Ahinadab
Mahanaim

Ahimaaz
Naphtali

Baanah
Asher, Aloth

Jehoshaphat
Issachar

Shimei
Benjamin

Geber
Gilead

*A*ll of the words below describe a key figure in the Bible. The vowels of the words are missing, however. When you add the vowels and fit the words into the grid, the name of this famous Bible person will be revealed.

JSTN (2 words)

WNDRFL

SRVNT

RRGHTSNSS (2 words)

CNSLR

KNGFTHJWS (4 words)

CHRST

VN

LPHNDMG (3 words)

PRNCFPC (3 words)

MNFSRRWS (3 words)

DYSPRNG

MDTR

BRGHTNDMRNNGSTR (4 words)

SHPHRD

41

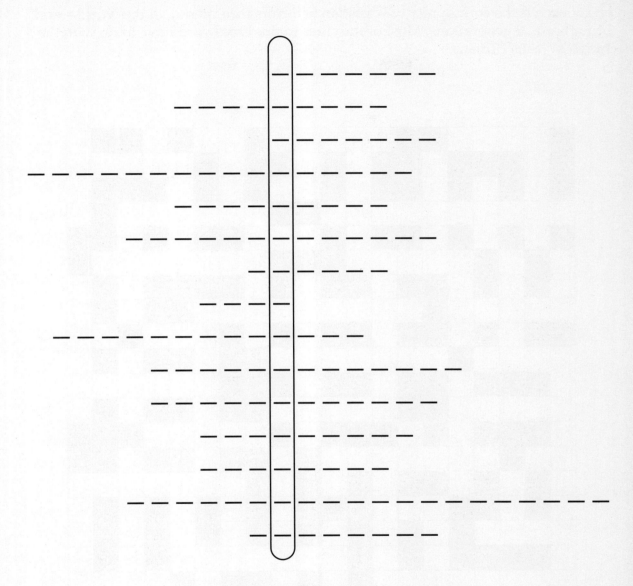

Scripture Pool

PSALM 80:1   ISAIAH 9:6; 52:13; 53:3   JEREMIAH 23:6   MATTHEW 2:2
LUKE 1:78   JOHN 15:5   ACTS 7:52   1 TIMOTHY 2:5   1 JOHN 5:1
REVELATION 22:13, 16

*T*he church is the community of Christian believers throughout all the world—and throughout all generations. Most of the clues in this crossword have to do with the church of Jesus Christ.

Across

1 "Enter by the narrow _____ " (Matthew 7:13)
2 The Greek term for *hell* (Matthew 16:18)
5 You and I
9 "The _____ , the Lamb's wife" (Revelation 21:9)
11 Extraterrestrial (abbr.)
12 "A holy _____ , to offer up spiritual sacrifices acceptable to God through Jesus Christ" (1 Peter 2:5)
13 The chief cornerstone of the church (Ephesians 2:20)
15 Before now
18 Disciples met together to "break _____ " (Acts 20:7)
20 "We are members of His body . . . This is a great _____ " (Ephesians 5:30, 32)
23 These people became members of the church (Acts 2:47)
24 Christians are members of the _____ of God (Ephesians 2:19)
26 The sick are instructed to call the leaders of the church for prayer and anointing with _____ (James 5:14)
27 Great persecution rose against the church which was "_____ Jerusalem" (Acts 8:1)
28 Stephen, one of the first deacons, was a man " _____ of faith and the Holy Spirit" (Acts 6:5)
29 Where disciples were first called Christians (Acts 11:26)
32 House of the Lord (Ephesians 2:21)
33 Husbands should love their wives as Christ _____ the church (Ephesians 5:25)
34 Paul admonished Christians to seek to "be skilled" in spiritual gifts for the edification of the church (1 Corinthians 14:12)
36 A righteous person (Ephesians 2:19)
37 " _____ this rock I will build My church" (Matthew 16:18)
38 "Individuals" who belong to the body of Christ (1 Corinthians 12:27)
44 Give praise (1 Corinthians 12:26)
47 When the church gathered together, they "reported all that _____ had done with them" (Acts 14:27)
48 The church should be " _____ and without blemish" (Ephesians 5:27)
50 "Not having spot or _____ " (Ephesians 5:27)
52 One of the offices of the church; these people had a special word from God for a particular circumstance (1 Corinthians 12:28)
53 The church met together to _____ (Acts 2:42)

Down

1 Honor and praise; the churches are the " _____ of Christ" (2 Corinthians 8:23)

3 Agreement (Acts 2:1)
4 "The _____ cannot say to the hand, 'I have no need of you'" (1 Corinthians 12:21)
5 " _____ one accord" (Acts 2:46)
6 "Where two _____ three are gathered together" (Matthew 18:20)
7 Authority (Colossians 2:19)
8 One of the apostles, his name means "Rock" (Matthew 16:18)
9 Jesus, the Cornerstone, and Christians, the living stones, are being _____ up into a spiritual house (1 Peter 2:5)
10 Allow (Colossians 3:15)
13 Early Christians "had all things in _____ " (Acts 2:44)
14 Christ is present where #49 Down or _____ meet in His name (Matthew 18:20)
16 "We are members of _____ body, of _____ flesh and of _____ bones" (Ephesians 5:30)
17 A bishop must have a good testimony "lest he fall into . . . the snare of the _____ " (1 Timothy 3:7)
18 "His _____ , which is the church" (Colossians 1:24)
19 One sent forth (1 Corinthians 12:28)
21 One who instructs (1 Corinthians 12:28)
22 "Assemble" together (Matthew 18:20)
25 Belief (Acts 2:42)
28 Koinonia, in Greek (Acts 2:42)
30 Inclined
31 "Believers were increasingly _____ to the Lord" (Acts 5:14)
35 Citizens' band (abbr.)
39 Spiritual leaders of the church (1 Timothy 5:17)
40 "Exalt Him al_____ in the assembly of the people" (Psalm 107:32)
41 "For by one _____ we were all baptized into one body" (1 Corinthians 12:13)
42 "The church of the living God, the _____ and ground of the truth" (1 Timothy 3:15)
43 "If one member suffers, _____ the members suffer with it; or if one member is honored, _____ the members rejoice with it" (1 Corinthians 12:26)
44 Petra, in Greek (Matthew 16:18)
45 This twenty-sixth book of the New Testament tells believers to "contend earnestly for the faith"
46 Build up; " _____ one another" (1 Thessalonians 5:11)
47 "Christ also loved the church and _____ Himself for her" (Ephesians 5:25)
49 See #14 Across
51 Behold (Revelation 7:9, KJV)

*D*iscover three of the most potent Bible verses for those who are under a great deal of stress!

Clue: MESSIAH *is* MSOOCIT

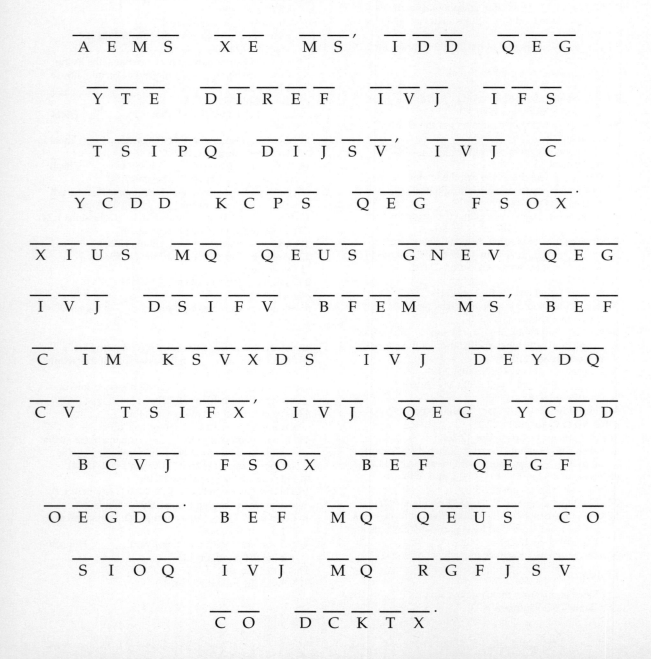

AEMS   XE   MS'   IDD   QEG

YTE   DIREF   IVJ   IFS

TSIPQ   DIJSV'   IVJ   C

YCDD   KCPS   QEG   FSOX.

XIUS   MQ   QEUS   GNEV   QEG

IVJ   DSIFV   BFEM   MS'   BEF

CIM   KSVXDS   IVJ   DEYDQ

CV   TSIFX'   IVJ   QEG   YCDD

BCVJ   FSOX   BEF   QEGF

OEGDO   BEF   MQ   QEUS   CO

SIOQ   IVJ   MQ   RGFJSV

CO   DCKTX.

*P*haraoh's refusal to allow the children of Israel to return to the promised land led to great misery for the Egyptian people. Below is a list of the ten plagues that fell on the Egyptians as a result of Pharaoh's stubbornness. After unscrambling the words, unscramble the circled letters to find out why Pharaoh refused to let the Israelites go.

LODOB   _ _ _ _ ⭕

GORFS   _ ⭕ _ _ _

CILE   _ _ _ ⭕

LIFES   _ _ _ ⭕ _

LICENSEPET   _ ⭕ _ _ _ _ _ ⭕ _ _

SOLIB   _ _ _ _ _

LAHI   ⭕⭕ _ _

CUTLOSS   _ _ _ _ _ ⭕ _

DRSNAKES   _ ⭕⭕ _ _ _ _ _

HATED   ⭕ _ _ _ ⭕

Scrambled letters:

_ _ _ _ _ _ _ _ _ _ _ _

Unscrambled letters:

_ _ _ _ _ _ _ _ _ _ _ _

Scripture Pool
EXODUS 7:17; 8:2, 16, 21; 9:3, 9, 18; 10:4, 21; 11:5

45

*F*ools have a lot to learn.

Across

1 God chose foolish things to shame the _____ (1 Corinthians 1:27)

4 Did the Corinthians think him a fool? (2 Corinthians 11:16)

6 A foolish woman is "loud" (Proverbs 9:13)

9 A foolish son is the "downfall" of his father (Proverbs 19:13)

11 Sixteenth U.S. President, for short

13 God knew this psalmist's foolishness (Psalm 69:5)

14 The "seer" is a fool, said Hosea, because of Israel's great sin (Hosea 9:7)

15 Foolish "desires" (1 Timothy 6:9)

18 Doing "wickedness" is sport to a fool (Proverbs 10:23)

19 A fool's "speaking tool" is near destruction (Proverbs 10:14)

21 God told Zechariah: Take the implements of a foolish "lamb leader" (Zechariah 11:15)

24 A foolish man "wastes" treasure (Proverbs 21:20)

28 Foolish for them to risk Eden's loss (3 words)

29 Saying, "You fool," brings danger of this fire (Matthew 5:22)

30 Shame is the "inheritance" of fools (Proverbs 3:35)

33 Storing up crops didn't save the rich man's _____ (Luke 12:20)

34 Doing this silences the ignorance of foolish men (1 Peter 2:15)

35 Would *you* build a house on this? (Matthew 7:26)

Down

2 Devising foolishness is "impiety" (Proverbs 24:9)

3 His wife spoke like a foolish woman (Job 2:10)

4 Postscript (abbr.)

5 Wisdom is too "high" for a fool (Proverbs 24:7)

7 This writer sought to know the wickedness of foolishness and "lunacy" (Ecclesiastes 7:25)

8 Don't make me the "disgrace" of the foolish, David said (Psalm 39:8)

10 God was angered by foolish "graven images" (Deuteronomy 32:21)

12 Foolish "purists" left inward parts dirty (Luke 11:39–40)

13 Avoid foolish "arguments" (2 Timothy 2:23)

16 Foolish Jacob and Judah, with eyes that couldn't _____ (Jeremiah 5:20–21)

17 A foolish man "hates" his mother (Proverbs 15:20)

20 Spreading "defamation" makes one a fool (Proverbs 10:18)

22 Foolishness "dirties" a man (Mark 7:20–23)

23 Men's foolish _____ were darkened (though still beating) (Romans 1:21)

25 Any fool can start a "fight" (Proverbs 20:3)

26 He's the biggest fool of all

27 This king played the fool with David (1 Samuel 26:21)

31 The fool doesn't believe in Him (Psalm 14:1)

32 No's antonym

Work the clues about the building of Solomon's temple to find the number of years it took to complete the temple. The answers are found in the book of 1 Kings in the chapter and verse at the end of each clue.

The number of Israelites in the labor force (5:13)

$=$ _____

Multiplied by . . .
The part of the wall that was the door
of the sanctuary (6:33)

$\times$ _____

Divided by . . .
The number of years after the children of Israel
left Egypt before Solomon began building the
temple (6:1)

$\div$ _____

Multiplied by . . .
The year of Solomon's reign when work on
the temple began (6:1)

$\times$ _____

Multiplied by . . .
The length of the temple in cubits (6:2)

$\times$ _____

Divided by . . .
The number of rows of hewn stone in the
inner court (6:36)

$\div$ _____

Multiplied by . . .
The width in cubits of the inner sanctuary (6:20)

$\times$ _____

Minus . . .
The number of construction supervisors (5:16)

$-$ _____

Divided by . . .
The width of the temple in cubits (6:2)

$\div$ _____

Multiplied by . . .
The number of cherubim in the inner sanctuary (6:23)

$\times$ _____

Minus . . .
The number of baths in the Sea (7:26)

$-$ _____

Plus . . .
The number of years that Solomon reigned
as king (11:42)

$+$ _____

Divided by . . .
The height in cubits of the temple (6:2)

$\div$ _____

Equals . . .
The number of years it took to build the temple (6:38)

$=$ _____

*T*here are twelve people named in this puzzle who are related in some way to Aaron, Israel's first high priest. Find the names of Aaron's great-grandfather, grandfather, father, mother, brother, sister, wife, sons, and grandson.

```
E  L  E  A  Z  P  H  I  M  A  R  M  A  K  O  L

R  O  M  I  R  I  A  M  A  M  R  J  O  C  R  E

D  O  J  R  A  H  I  H  M  A  I  A  M  V  A  V

E  K  O  H  A  V  T  O  R  T  B  B  I  E  M  O

B  O  C  A  E  M  S  A  A  E  Z  I  R  L  A  S

E  B  H  L  P  E  H  A  H  A  P  H  I  N  H  A

H  H  A  M  S  O  R  S  D  O  A  U  A  A  T  M

C  S  B  D  I  M  I  A  H  O  K  E  N  B  I  H

O  I  E  A  A  L  N  S  O  M  O  S  E  I  D  I

J  L  D  H  E  N  V  E  L  E  B  E  H  C  O  J

B  E  A  T  S  R  A  Z  A  E  L  E  L  H  A  R

O  P  H  I  N  E  H  A  S  R  I  M  E  U  N  I

M  I  R  I  A  D  A  N  B  E  H  S  I  L  E  A
```

Scripture Pool
EXODUS 6:16, 18, 20, 23, 25 (KJV); 7:1; 15:20

48

We are told to fear God—to respect and acknowledge who He is. But we really don't have to be afraid.

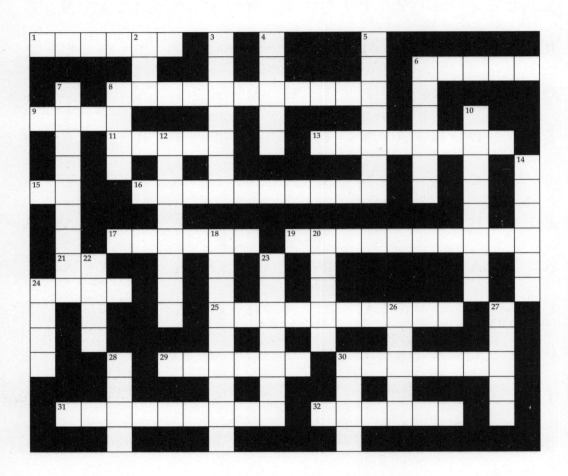

Across

1 Fearing Jezebel, he ran (1 Kings 19:1–3)

6 "Only fear the LORD, and serve Him in 'honesty'" (1 Samuel 12:24)

8 Fearing the approaching Moabites and Ammonites, this king of Judah proclaimed a fast (2 Chronicles 20:1–3)

9 "The fear of the LORD is a fountain of 'being'" (Proverbs 14:27)

11 Fear not, Jacob; God pours _____ on the thirsty (Isaiah 44:2–3)

13 God said not to fear the gods of these "mountain dwellers" (Judges 6:10)

15 Joshua wasn't to fear this royal city of Canaan (Joshua 8:1)

16 Peter feared the "rambunctious" wind (Matthew 14:29–30)

17 "Reprimand" sinners publicly, that others may also fear (1 Timothy 5:20)

19 Walking in the fear of the Lord, the churches "increased" (Acts 9:31)

21 _____ Shaddai

24 Jacob feared an encounter with him (Genesis 32:11)

25 Even these obeyed Him, though the Twelve feared them (3 words) (Mark 4:40–41)

29 The angel told Paul not to fear, that he must appear before this emperor (Acts 27:24)

30 God parted the Red Sea so the Israelites would fear God "through eternity" (Joshua 4:23–24)

31 The blind man's parents feared being put out of this place (John 9:22)

32 When Benjamin's mother was in hard labor, the midwife told her not to fear (Genesis 35:16–17)

Down

2 Wonder, reverence (Psalm 119:161)

3 "He will fulfill the 'longing' [pl.] of those who fear Him" (Psalm 145:19)

4 Did the people not fear God because He held His _____ ? (Isaiah 57:11)

5 Fear is due the King of the "republics" (Jeremiah 10:7)

6 A man who fears God isn't afraid of evil "news" (sing.) (Psalm 112:7)

7 They were afraid of the notorious Saul when he tried to join them (Acts 9:26)

8 Shutting the doors for fear of these people, the disciples met and had a surprise visit from Jesus (John 20:19)

10 The scribes and chief priests feared Jesus because His "instruction" amazed the people (Mark 11:18)

12 "Let not your heart be _____ " (John 14:27)

14 "The fear of the LORD is the beginning of _____ " (Proverbs 9:10)

18 Another word for #14 Down, from Proverbs 1:7

20 David was afraid to move the ark after God struck down this man (2 Samuel 6:6–10)

22 Don't be afraid, said Jesus; "I am the First and the _____ " (Revelation 1:17)

23 Those who feared death were subject to "enslavement" (Hebrews 2:15)

24 Fear of the Lord is to hate "wickedness" (Proverbs 8:13)

26 Fear of being killed made Abraham claim she was only his sister (Genesis 20:2, 11)

27 "So great is His _____ toward those who fear Him" (Psalm 103:11)

28 "Fear God. Honor the _____ ." (1 Peter 2:17)

30 The subject of this puzzle

TO TOUCH JESUS

*O*ne can imagine the crowds of people that followed and surrounded Jesus as He taught and healed those who came to Him. A person probably had to be rather able-bodied to even get close to Him. But a woman who had been ill for twelve years would have to be even more determined.

Apparently having given up any hope of encountering Jesus face to face, this sick but unwavering woman believed that if she could just touch the hem of His garment, she would be healed. So that is what she decided to do. But getting to Jesus was not easy. She maybe even had to crawl along the ground around and between the feet of those standing between her and her Master. Her faith and persistence were rewarded when she touched Jesus' garment. Jesus turned to her and said, "Daughter, be of good cheer; your faith has made you well." (See Luke 8:43-48.)

Unable to fight the crowd, a certain woman crawled along the ground to touch the hem of Jesus' garment. Find the path to Jesus without stepping on any feet.

*U*nscramble the names of these Bible people, and then unscramble the circled letters to reveal what they had in common. (See how many you can unscramble before consulting the Scripture Pool.)

BOACJ   _ Ⓞ _ _ _

ONHA   _ _ _ _

BRAAMAH   Ⓞ _ _ _ _ _ _

SEMOS   _ _ _ _ _

JILHEA   _ Ⓞ _ _ _ _

children of
EBRUNE / DGA   Ⓞ _ _ _ _ _ / _ _ _   (2 words)

VELTISE   _ _ _ _ Ⓞ _ _

Unscrambled letters:

_ _ _ _ _

Scripture Pool

GENESIS 8:20   GENESIS 22:9   GENESIS 33:18, 20   GENESIS 35:6–7
EXODUS 17:15   JOSHUA 22:34   1 KINGS 18:30–32   EZEKIEL 43:19–20

The apostle Peter was not a man without problems!

Across

3 Where Peter found money (Matthew 17:27)

5 Rose of _____ (Song of Solomon 2:1)

7 "It is hard for a _____ man to enter the kindgom of heaven" (Matthew 19:23)

8 Nickname for a physician

9 Peter's other name (Matthew 10:2)

11 _____ California; Mexican peninsula

13 Christ built this "on this rock" (Matthew 16:18)

15 Preposition

16 Either's partner

17 A direction for the wind to blow (abbr.)

18 Where Herod put Peter (Acts 12:5)

21 Peter's liberator (Acts 12:7)

23 Sweet potato

25 Number of times Peter denied Christ (Luke 22:61)

26 "Come unto _____ "

27 " _____ who believes and is baptized will be saved" (Mark 16:16)

29 Loaves and fishes containers (Matthew 14:20)

30 Occupation of Peter's Joppa host (Acts 9:43)

33 "In the beginning was the ____" (John 1:1)

34 "Behold, I stand at the ____ and knock" (Revelation 3:20)

36 Spirit of a person

38 When Peter escaped from prison, she got so excited that she forgot to answer the door (Acts 12:13)

39 Number of times the cock crowed (Mark 14:72)

42 Maryland neighbor (abbr.)

43 Stay

45 "And by His ____ we are healed" (Isaiah 53:5)

48 Easter exultation: "He is ____!"

49 John 7:24: "Do not judge according to ____, "

52 Hospital's life-sustaining tube (abbr.)

53 Manhattan's home state (abbr.)

54 Twelve hours past midnight

55 Tidings

56 Gratuity, lead, or topmost part

57 He crowed twice (Mark 14:72)

Down

1 Wealthy

2 Here and ____

3 Peter's occupation (John 21:3)

4 Some of the animals in Peter's vision had this kind of foot

5 Multiplied by itself

6 Close by

7 "And on this ____ I will build My church" (Matthew 16:18)

10 What Peter found in the mouth of the fish (Matthew 17:27)

12 What an Old Testament fish found in his mouth!

14 What Peter called the animals in his vision (Acts 10:14)

19 Animal-holder in Peter's vision (Acts 10:11)

20 "____ one of the least of these" (Matthew 25:40, KJV)

22 Christ, the ____ of God (John 1:29)

24 Size up

27 He put Peter in prison (Acts 12:1–4)

28 "Many are called, but ____ are chosen" (Matthew 20:16)

30 "One" follower

31 Tuber

32 One of Peter's fellow sleepers at Gethsemane (Mark 14:33)

34 Creed

35 Desert garden

36 Occupation of Peter's accuser (Mark 14:69)

37 Yeast

40 Victor

41 Popular crunchy cheese snack (sing.)

42 Jesus predicted Peter would do this to Him (Mark 14:72)

44 Location of Dan's tribe in relationship to the tabernacle (Numbers 2:25)

46 Body of flowing water

47 Pig places

50 Hawaiian root-paste dish

51 Nickname for Dad

*D*ecipher the message below to see what the Lord had to say in relation to the object of puzzle #50!

Clue: MESSIAH *is* GCJJEAQ

E T   C X C V M   U S A B C

L Q C V C   E V C B H V O

G M   T A G C   E

L E S S   B H G C   W H

M H K ' A T O   E L E S S

N S C J J   M H K .

C Y H O K J   20:24

LITTLE CHILDREN

*M*atthew 19:13–15 gives us an account of Jesus' relationship to children. One can imagine that a young mother must have ventured forth with a small child to seek Jesus' blessing . . . and then perhaps another and another until Jesus was surrounded by the little ones. His disciples, seeking to protect Him from the "annoyance" of so many children, rebuked them and shooed them away. But Jesus said, "Let the little children come to Me, and do not forbid them; for of such is the kingdom of heaven" (v.14).

Gather all the children and take them to Jesus. Travel each path only once, and do not cross over your own path.

*M*any of the clues for this puzzle relate to the third personage of the Trinity.

Across

1 Two regions where "you shall be witnesses to Me" (use *and* between) (Acts 1:8)

11 Angel's hat

12 What the Holy Spirit gives (Acts 1:8)

14 Another name: Holy _____

18 Author Eliot's first two initials

19 What sat upon the Upper Room occupants (3 words) (Acts 2:3)

24 Get up

25 Entice

26 Govern

27 Comes before "dos"

28 Speechless

30 Not false

31 Bride and groom's word

33 Initials of the light-bulb man

34 Had dinner

35 Hear-piece

36 Holy Spirit came to Jesus in this form (Luke 3:22)

37 John the Baptist baptized Him (Luke 3:21)

40 Name for a Norseman

42 Salem, Eugene, and Portland state (abbr.)

43 Bean's cousin
47 Place for pigs
48 Soft, light metal
49 "For God so ____ the world" (John 3:16)
51 Him's counterpart
52 What the Holy Spirit makes us (Acts 1:8)
54 Bond
57 Name of a false god; an Olympian
59 Attorney's professional group
60 Day of Pentecost preacher (Acts 2:14)
61 He will also be the reaper (2 Corinthians 9:6)

Down
 2 Sound of pleasure
 3 Chart
 4 Paraclete: One who comes ____ to help
 5 Continuous succession
 6 Free-floating gas
 7 Old's opposite
 8 Earthenware container of liquid
 9 Pair (slang)
10 Biblical location of day of Pentecost account (2 words)
13 Twilight time of day
15 Rabbit
16 Frequent designation for early Christians (sing., abbr.) (Romans 1:7)
17 Another name for the Holy Spirit (John 14:26, KJV)
20 Circles result if both aren't in the water
21 What the Spirit produces in Christians (Galatians 5:22)
22 "But be ____ with the Spirit" (Ephesians 5:18)
23 "I once was blind, but now ____ ____" (2 words) "Amazing Grace"
27 "As the Spirit gave them ____" (Acts 2:4)
29 Main part of the church sanctuary
32 Horse's favorite type of bran
37 Peter quoted this prophet in his sermon (Acts 2:16)
38 They were awaiting the Holy Spirit in the ____ Room (Acts 1:13)
39 Plant starter
41 "Suddenly there ____ a sound from heaven" (Acts 2:2)
44 Article
45 John did this with water (present tense) (John 1:31)
46 Upper arm bone
50 Bible division
52 Put on
53 A special one appeared in the East
55 Opposite of down
56 Extraterrestrial of movie fame
58 "____ send I you" (John 20:21, KJV)
59 "To ____ or not to ____" (Shakespeare)

Connect the letters below into a word string to reveal one of Jesus' harshest sayings in the entire New Testament. See how many letters you can connect before consulting the reference at the base of the chalice, or "cup."

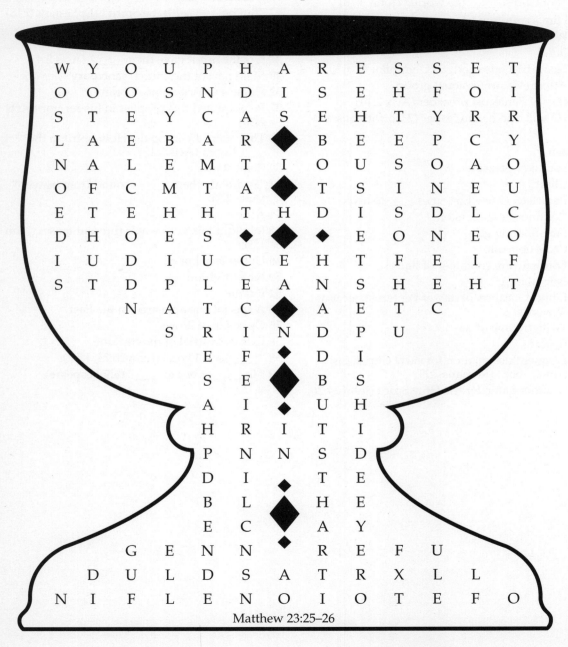

Matthew 23:25–26

Good instructions for Christian living.

Clue: MESSIAH *is* COMMAND

P O Y U A W O   N B X N S M '

Z P N S   X A E D U L E

W O N M A H I ' A H

O G O P S E D A H I   I A G O

E D N H F M ;   Q U P   E D A M

A M   E D O   X A B B U Q

I U R   A H   W D P A M E

Y O M L M   Q U P   S U L .

THE FIFTH DAY

*T*he maze depicts some of the things that God created on the fifth day. God's creation of the universe was a very orderly process. First He created the environment that the living creatures needed in order to survive and multiply. Then He created the creatures themselves.

On the fifth day the Lord made the creatures of the sky and the sea. The animals in this maze are an angelfish, whale, seahorse, bird, chick, frog, snail, starfish, and dove.

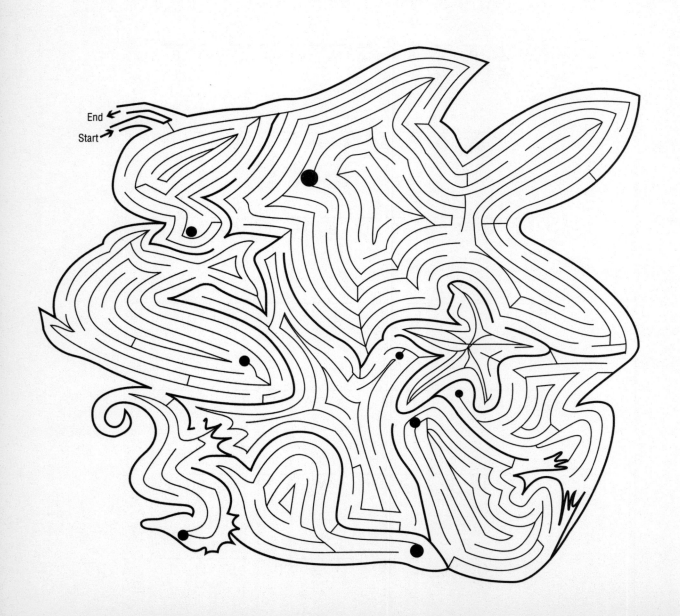

Revelation is a book in which numbers abound—frequently as symbols. Using the numbers indicated by the clues, work the equation to come up with the "perfect" answer. All the numbers are found in the book of Revelation. You may need your calculator for this one!

Number of Jews receiving the seal of the living God
(Revelation 7:4)   =   _____

Divided by . . .
Number equal to ten percent of the army of the horsemen
(Revelation 9:16)   ÷   _____

Multiplied by . . .
Number of men killed in the earthquake after the
murdered prophets ascended (Revelation 11:13)   ×   _____

Minus . . .
Number of living creatures (full of eyes) surrounding the
throne (Revelation 4:6)   —   _____

Divided by . . .
Number of edges on the sword coming from the Son of
man's mouth (Revelation 1:16)   ÷   _____

Multiplied by . . .
Number of months locusts were allowed to sting
(Revelation 9:5)   ×   _____

Plus . . .
Number of thrones around God's throne (Revelation 4:4)   +   _____

Divided by . . .
Number of lampstands (Revelation 2:1)   ÷   _____

Plus . . .
Number of pearls used for each gate in the New Jerusalem
(Revelation 21:21)   +   _____

Divided by . . .
Number of gates on each wall of New Jerusalem
(Revelation 21:13)   ÷   _____

Number of churches that received the Revelation from
John (Revelation 1:4)   =   _____

*N*ot all the authors of the Bible are known for sure, but the ones that are known come from a wide variety of walks of life. They include a fisherman, poet, musician, prophet, priest, and king. Using your Bible and Bible concordance, find the answers to the clues in this crossword and fill in the grid.

Word Pool

AGUR AMOS ASAPH DANIEL DAVID ETHAN EZEKIEL EZRA
HABAKKUK HAGGAI HEMAN HOSEA ISAIAH JAMES JEREMIAH
JOEL JOHN JONAH JUDE SONS OF <u>KORAH</u> LEMUEL LUKE
MALACHI MARK MATTHEW MICAH MOSES NAHUM NEHEMIAH
OBADIAH PAUL PETER SOLOMON ZECHARIAH ZEPHANIAH

Across

2 He went naked to carry his prophetic message; a prophet from the town of Moresheth

4 A prophet of royal descent, he was the great-great-grandson of King Hezekiah

7 Priest, scribe, expert in the words of the commandments of the Lord

8 Son of Pethuel, author of one of the books of the minor prophets

9 Patriarch of the Exodus

10 Musician, shepherd, warrior, and king

11 A prophet, he wrote about the destruction coming to Edom

13 Tax collector and disciple

15 Physician and disciple

18 Contributor to the book of Proverbs

19 Son of Hilkiah, he was a prophet from Anathoth

20 Herdsman from Tekoa

23 Son of Berechiah and grandson of Iddo, he wrote a book of the minor prophets

26 Called "the Ezrahite," he wrote a psalm (1 Chronicles 15:19)

27 His name is mentioned only once in Scripture as the author of the last book in the Old Testament

28 This Ezrahite wrote a favorite psalm—"I will sing of the mercies of the LORD forever"

29 A prophet from Judah, the theme of his book is "the just shall live by his faith"

30 As a captive in Babylon, he was called Belteshazzar

Down

1 The brother of the Lord wrote this book as a letter to the "twelve tribes which are scattered abroad"

3 A priest in charge of the singers, he wrote several psalms (1 Chronicles 15:19)

5 Tentmaker and apostle to the Gentiles

6 Son of Beeri, faithful husband to Gomer, and father of Jezreel, Lo-Ruhamah, and Lo-Ammi

7 A priest, the son of Buzi

8 "Bondservant of Jesus Christ, and brother of James," he wrote a warning about false teachers

12 Fisherman and disciple

13 A Gospel writer, disciple, and missionary traveler with Paul and Barnabas

14 This son of Amoz wrote a book that bears his name; it records a vision from the Lord concerning Judah and Jerusalem

16 A music guild of singers and composers credited with writing ten psalms

17 An Elkoshite, this prophet foretold the fall of the city of Nineveh

19 The beloved disciple

21 Wise king

22 Cupbearer to Artaxerxes I

24 A king who contributed to the book of Proverbs

25 Son of Amittal, a prophet who was from Gath Hepher

26 Author of a book of the minor prophets, he prophesied of Joshua to Zerubbabel

God's encouraging word to Joshua is still a good word of encouragement to us today.

Clue: MESSIAH *is* CRIISTO

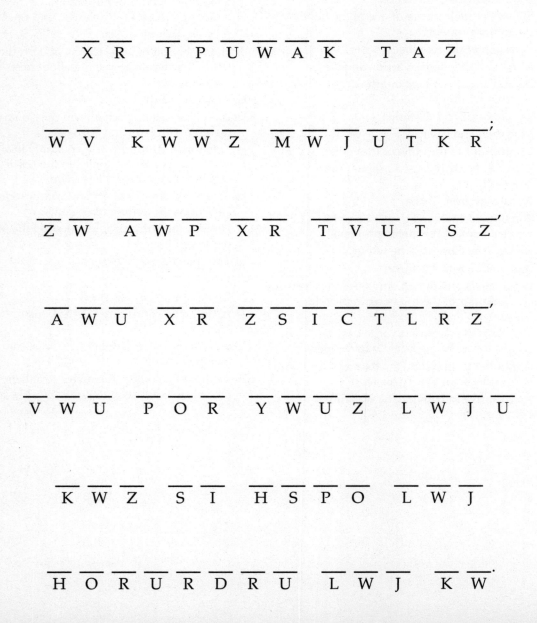

X R   I P U W A K   T A Z

W V   K W W Z   M W J U T K R ;

Z W   A W P   X R   T V U T S Z '

A W U   X R   Z S I C T L R Z '

V W U   P O R   Y W U Z   L W J U

K W Z   S I   H S P O   L W J

H O R U R D R U   L W J   K W .

THE OPEN WORD

*T*he Bible is the most widely read book in the world. It continues to appear on the list of best-selling books every year. Yet owning a Bible does not assure its owner of a relationship with God.

The book of John says, "In the beginning was the Word, and the Word was with God, and the Word was God. . . .And the Word became flesh and dwelt among us, and we beheld His glory, the glory as of the only begotten of the Father, full of grace and truth" (v. 1, 14).

The Word of God is not just a beautiful piece of literature or an historical account of our spiritual roots, it is literally the Word of God to us and our path to Him through Jesus Christ His Son.

Start at "In the beginning" and finish at "Amen."

*U*nscramble the words below, all of which have something in common.

TIHEW   __ __ __ ◯ __   (Revelation 6:2)

LABKC   __ __ ▢ __ __   (Revelation 6:5)

ERGNE   ▢ __ __ __ ◇   (Psalm 23:2)

RICOMSN   __ __ ◯ __ ◇ __ __   (Isaiah 1:18)

PULERP   __ ◯ __ __ __ __   (Judges 8:26)

LEBU   __ __ __ ◇   (Exodus 28:31)

ELAP   __ __ ▢ __   (Revelation 6:8)

ERD   __ ▢ __   (Revelation 6:4)

LERACST   ◇ ◯ __ __ __ __ ◇   (Nahum 2:3)

NOLGDE   __ ◇ __ __ __ __   (Exodus 28:34)

LEOYWL   __ ▢ __ __ __ __   (Leviticus 13:30)

OBRNW   __ __ __ __ ◯   (Genesis 30:32)

YGAR   __ __ __ __   (Deuteronomy 32:25)

Unscramble the marked letters above to reveal
three items the Bible describes as being of "many":

The CIRCLED letters   __ __ __ __ __   (Genesis 37:3)

The DIAMOND letters   __ __ __ __ __ __   (1 Chronicles 29:2)

The SQUARE letters   __ __ __ __ __   (Ezekiel 17:3)

"*H*e counts the number of the stars; He calls them all by name. Great is our Lord, and mighty in power; His understanding is infinite" (Psalm 147:4–5).

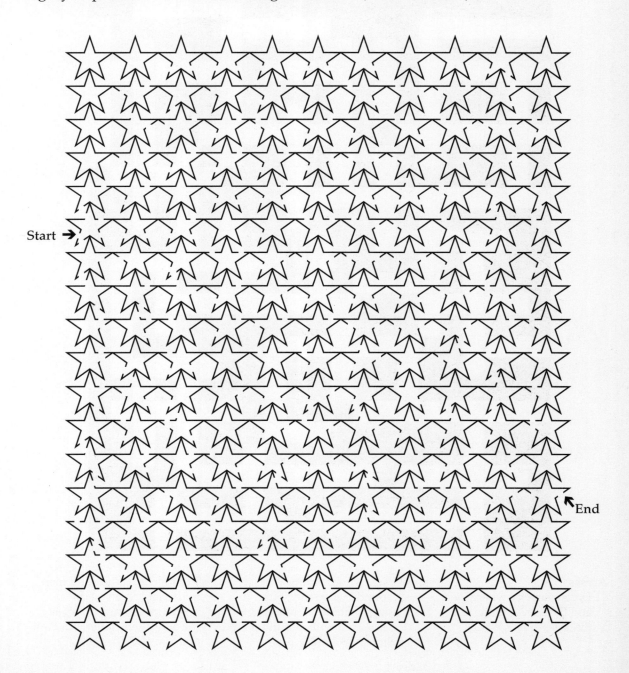

*P*eople and places of the early church form the words of this crossword grid. All of the references are from Acts.

Across

1 Lycaonian city where Paul and Barnabas "made many disciples" (14:6, 20–21)

2 Place where Philip was "found" when the Spirit caught him away after his discussion with an Ethiopian eunuch (8:39–40)

4 Prominent women and men in this city received the gospel when they searched the Scriptures daily with Paul and Silas (17:10–12)

9 Paul taught daily for two years in the one established by Tyrannus in Ephesus (19:9–10)

11 Paul preached to the people of this city while standing in the midst of the Aeropagus (17:22)

12 Place where disciples were first called Christians (11:26)

14 Region of a second "Antioch"; Paul and Barnabas shook the dust of this city from their feet when the people refused to accept the gospel (13:13–52)

15 Both Jewish and Greek communities were split over the gospel in this city; both Jews and Greeks attempted to abuse Paul and Barnabas (14:1–5)

18 Woman from Thyatira who opened her me to Paul in Philippi (16:11–15)

19 This city's rulers called Paul and Silas those "who have turned the world upside down" (17:1–9)

22 Apollos vigorously debated the Jews there and "greatly helped those who had believed" (18:24–28)

25 Philip's home city, where he lived with his four daughters who prophesied (21:8–9)

28 Crete or Malta, for example

29 Many in this city believed in the Lord after Peter raised Tabitha from the dead (9:36–42)

30 Paul met with James and the elders of this city about conformity by Gentiles to Jewish customs (21)

31 A slave, she was delivered by Paul from a spirit of divination (16:16–18)

32 The ruler of the synagogue in Corinth who became a believer (18:8)

35 Many were healed, including Publius's father, during Paul's shipwreck stay on this island (28:1–10)

37 Wife of Aquila, she worked with Paul and helped train Apollos (18:1–3, 26)

39 The people here turned to the Lord after seeing the healing of a paralyzed man (9:35)

40 Person Paul saw in a vision saying, "Come over to Macedonia and help us" (16:9)

42 Prophet from Judea who took Paul's belt and bound his hands and feet, prophesying Paul's arrest in Jerusalem (21:10–11)

43 A Greek believer in Athens called "the Areopagite" (17:34)

45 He fell from a third-story window while Paul was preaching and was restored to life (20:9–12)

46 Region in which Paul traveled, "strengthening all he disciples" (18:23)

Down

1 While on the road to persecute believers in this city, Saul heard the voice of the Lord in a blinding light (9:1–9)

3 The first place Paul, Barnabas, and John Mark preached the gospel in Jewish synagogues after being sent out from the Antiochian church (13:5)

5 The Lord "worked unusual miracles by the hands of Paul" in this city, even using Paul's handkerchiefs and aprons to heal the sick (19:11–12)

6 Believers met in her house in Jerusalem to pray for Peter's release from prison (12:12)

7 The rulers of this city asked Paul and Silas to leave after imprisoning them and then discovering they were Roman citizens (16:35–39)

8 A devout centurion in the Italian regiment, his conversion opened the gospel to the Gentile world in a dramatic way (10)

10 The Lord spoke to Paul in the night about this city and said, "Do not be afraid, but speak, and do not keep silent; for I am with you, and no one will attack you to hurt you; for I have many people in this city" (18:9–10)

13 Charitable woman also known as Tabitha, whom Peter raised from the dead (9:36–41)

16 Girl who forgot to open the gate for Peter in her excitement at hearing his voice (12:13–16)

17 Place where Paul was stoned and left for dead until "the disciples gathered around him" (14:19–20)

20 Disciple in Damascus who laid hands on Saul, praying his sight would be restored and he would be filled with the Holy Spirit (9:10–18)

21 After Paul cast out evil spirits in the name of Jesus, this Jewish priest's seven sons attempted to cast out a demon in the name of Jesus, but they were wounded and had to flee (19:14–20)

23 "Lame" man; his healing in Lystra nearly caused a riot (14:6–18)

24 Paul stayed seven days with believers there en route to Jerusalem; they warned Paul "through the Spirit" not to go (21:3–6)

26 Paul spent two years in this city, preaching and teaching those who came to his "rented house" (28:30–31)

27 A fellow tentmaker, Paul stayed and worked with him while he was in Corinth (18:1–3)

30 Believer with whom Paul and Silas stayed in Thessalonica (17:5–9)

32 Paul perceived his vision of a Macedonian man as this from the Lord (16:10)

33 A tanner in Joppa, he opened his home to Peter (10:6)

34 Athenian woman who believed the gospel after hearing Paul preach of the resurrection (17:31–34)

36 Paul preached there for seven days, and on the final day, preached to and talked with the disciples all night (20:6–11)

38 Believer from Berea who accompanied Paul on his journey to Asia (20:4)

41 Tychicus and Trophimus, who worked closely with Paul, were believers from this region (20:4)

44 Abbreviated name of a disciple in Lystra who became a "true son in the faith" to Paul (16:1; 1 Timothy 1:2)

THE EMBATTLED CROSS

*T*his variation of the Greek cross (in which all four arms of the cross are equal in length) suggests the battlements of a fortress. It is an emblem of the Church Militant, a church ardently engaged in the defeat of the devil and his minions.

When used as part of liturgical vestments, the cross is worked in purple, indicating triumph through difficult times of battle.

The cross reminds us of Jesus' words to Peter: "On this rock I will build My church, and the gates of Hades shall not prevail against it" (Matthew 16:18).

Start

← End

Jesus used these words to comfort His disciples.

Clue: MESSIAH is AYZZXNF

W Y U   P K U   I K R G

F Y N G U   D Y

U G K R D W Y S ;   I K R

D Y W X Y H Y

X P   M K S '   D Y W X Y H Y

N W Z K   X P   A Y .

Can you hear the lion's roar?

Across

1 A young lion

3 When you make the Lord our refuge, "you shall ____ upon the lion and the cobra" (Psalm 91:13)

6 God replied to Jeremiah, "My ____ is to Me like a lion . . . it cries out against Me" (Jeremiah 12:8)

9 Prophet saved from a den of lions

10 "Blessed is he who ____ Gad; He dwells as a lion" (Deuteronomy 33:20)

14 The valiant are said to have the _____ of a lion (2 Samuel 17:10)

16 Lion's "crown"

17 Weapon of shepherd for fending off wild beasts

18 The Lord says of transgressors, "Your sword has _____ your prophets like a destroying lion" (Jeremiah 2:30)

19 "Judah is a lion's _____" (Genesis 49:9)

21 Hezekiah said of the Lord, "Like a lion, so He breaks all my _____" (Isaiah 38:13)

23 Sound a lion makes

24 The psalmist prayed for deliverance from persecutors "lest they _____ me like a lion" (Psalm 7:2)

25 "A swarm of bees and _____ were in the carcass of the lion" (Judge 14:8)

26 The psalmist prayed for deliverance from the lion's mouth and the _____ of wild oxen (Psalm 22:21)

28 The way a lion waits in his den (Psalm 10:9)

31 The one who enlarges _____ "dwells as a lion" (Deuteronomy 33:20)

33 A nearby lion's roar might make this seem to tremble

34 "The _____ man saith, 'There is a lion without, I shall be slain in the streets'" (Proverbs 22:13, KJV)

36 The king's _____ is described as being like the "roaring of a lion" (Proverbs 19:12)

38 Job said to God, "You hunt me like a _____ lion" (Job 10:16)

40 "Will a lion roar in the forest, when he has no _____?" (Amos 3:4)

42 Paul was delivered out of the _____ of the lion (2 Timothy 4:17)

43 "The lion has come up from his _____," says Jeremiah 4:7

Down

2 He killed a lion in a pit on a snowy day (2 Samuel 23:20)

3 Joel described the enemy as having the "_____ of a lion" (Joel 1:6)

4 Peter wrote, "Your _____ the devil walks bout like a roaring lion" (1 Peter 5:8)

5 Lion's home

7 "The _____ are bold as a lion" (Proverbs 28:1)

8 Daniel saw four great beasts: the first was like a lion that had the wings of an _____ (Daniel 7:4)

9 "A living dog is better than a _____ lion" (Ecclesiastes 9:4)

11 The devil "walks _____ like a roaring lion, seeking whom he may devour" (1 Peter 5:8)

12 The Lord regarded His heritage as a "lion in the _____" (Jeremiah 12:8)

13 The remnant of this tribe is described as a lion among the Gentiles (Micah 5:8)

15 David slew a lion and a _____ before acing Goliath

20 Female lion

22 He posed a riddle about a lion (Judges 14:12–14, 18)

27 "The king's wrath is like the _____ of a lion" (Proverbs 19:12)

29 It housed a swarm of bees and honey (Judges 14:8)

30 Jesus was described as the _____ of the tribe of Judah

32 Paul said, "I was _____ out of the mouth of the lion" (2 Timothy 4:17)

35 Joel described the enemy as having the "fangs of a _____ lion" (Joel 1:6)

37 The lion is called "_____ among beasts" in Proverbs 30:30

39 "The young lion and the _____ you shall trample underfoot" (Psalm 91:13)

41 A lion's search for food

FLIGHT ACROSS THE CITY

"*T*hen all the disciples forsook Him and fled" (Matthew 26:56).

Jesus had been betrayed by Judas Iscariot. Equally painful for Him must have been the desertion by Peter, James, and John, the three disciples who were with Him that night in the Garden of Gethsemane. But He understood their confusion and fear, and knew they were running from the situation—not from Him. They had much to learn about the cost of discipleship.

Future events proved that Jesus' faith in them was not misplaced.

Peter, James, and John must cross the city without entering the sections where the chief priests and Pharisees wait.

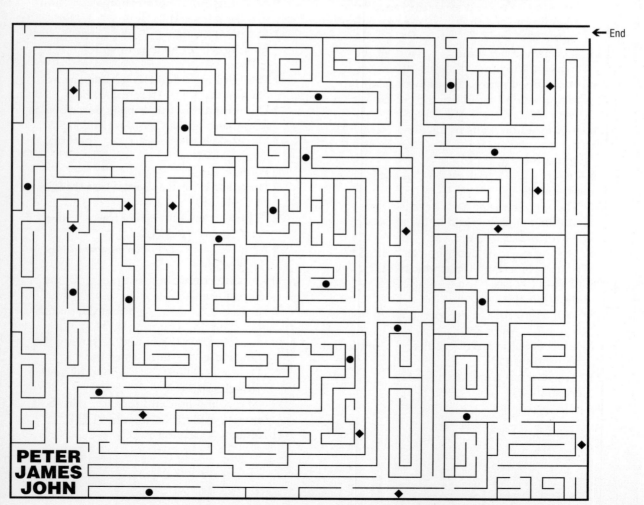

Confidence and assurance characterize the Christian faith.

Clue: MESSIAH *is* NRXXTEL

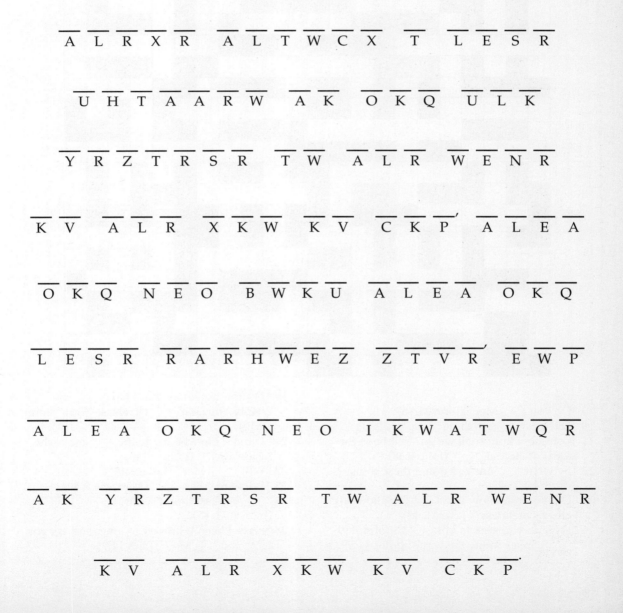

A L R X R   A L T W C X T   T   L E S R

U H T A A R W   A K   O K Q   U L K

Y R Z T R S R   T W   A L R   W E N R

K V   A L R   X K W   K V   C K P'   A L E A

O K Q   N E O   B W K U   A L E A   O K Q

L E S R   R A R H W E Z   Z T V R'   E W P

A L E A   O K Q   N E O   I K W A T W Q R

A K   Y R Z T R S R   T W   A L R   W E N R

K V   A L R   X K W   K V   C K P.

Questions . . . the Gospels are full of them. The disciples asking sincere questions, the Sadducees and Pharisees trying to ask the trick questions, Jesus asking questions to teach and examine persons' hearts. If Jesus was physically present on earth and you could ask Him any question, what would it be? What would you answer if Jesus asked *you*, "What do you want Me to do?"

Across

3 "Do you _____ Me?" (John 21:16)

9 "Did you _____ anything?" (Luke 22:35)

11 "Lord, to whom shall we go? You have the words of eternal _____" (John 6:68)

13 "By what _____ are You doing these things?" (Matthew 21:23)

15 "Did you not know that I _____ be about My Father's business?" (Luke 2:49)

16 "Why do you seek to kill _____?" (John 7:19)

17 "_____ can we know the way?" (John 14:5)

19 "Do You not know that I have _____ to crucify You, and _____ to release You?" (John 19:10)

21 "Did not He who made the _____ make the inside also?" (Luke 11:40)

22 "Who _____ Me?" (Luke 8:45)

23 "Why are you _____?" (Matthew 8:26)

26 "_____ makest thou thyself?" (John 8:53, KJV)

28 "Have I been with you so long, and yet you have not _____ Me?" (John 14:9)

29 "Who ____, this man or his parents, that he was born blind?" (John 9:2)

30 "Which is ____, the gold or the temple that sanctifies the gold?" (Matthew 23:17)

31 "What is your ____?" (Luke 8:30)

33 "Is this not the ____ son?" (Matthew 13:55)

37 "Are you ____?" (John 1:21)

39 "Do you suppose that I came to give ____ on earth?" (Luke 12:51)

41 "What profit is it to a man if he gains the ____ world, and loses his own soul?" (Matthew 16:26)

45 "Whom ____ you seeking?" (John 18:4)

46 "Whose ____ and inscription is this?" (Matthew 22:20)

47 "____ do you sleep?" (Luke 22:46)

48 "What is ____?" (John 18:38)

50 "Is it lawful for a man to ____ his wife for just any reason?" (Matthew 19:3)

51 "What will be the ____ of Your coming?" (Matthew 24:3)

52 "How then does he now ____?" (John 9:19)

55 "Have you any ____ here?" (Luke 24:41)

56 "Do you ____ in the Son of God?" (John 9:35)

58 "Who ____ forgive sins but God alone?" (Mark 2:7)

59 "Do you believe that I am ____ to do this?" (Matthew 9:28)

60 "Why do you call Me ____?" (Matthew 19:17)

61 "Are You the ____, or do we look for another?" (2 words) (Matthew 11:3)

Down

1 "If the salt has lost its ____, how shall it be seasoned?" (Luke 14:34)

2 "Why, what evil has ____ done?" (Matthew 27:23)

4 "Why does your Teacher ____ with tax collectors and sinners?" (Matthew 9:11)

5 "Rabbi, is ____ I?" (Matthew 26:25)

6 "Why ____ you call Me 'Lord, Lord,' and not do the things which I say?" (Luke 6:46)

7 "Why could not we cast ____ out?" (Mark 9:28, KJV)

8 "If I cast out demons ____ Beelzebub, ____ whom do your sons cast them out?" (Matthew 12:27)

10 "How then will his ____ stand?" (Matthew 12:26)

12 "O you of little ____, why did you doubt?" (Matthew 14:31)

14 "Why do you ____ Me, you hypocrites?" (Matthew 22:18)

17 "Could you not watch with Me one ____?" (Matthew 26:40)

18 "Where then do You get that ____ water?" (John 4:11)

20 "What shall we do, that we may work the ____ of God?" (John 6:28)

23 "Lord, are You washing my ____?" (John 13:6)

24 "But if you love those who love you, what ____ is that to you?" (Luke 6:32)

25 "Does your Teacher not pay the ____ tax?" (Matthew 17:24)

26 "Do you ____ to be made well?" (John 5:6)

27 "Whom do you want me to release to you? Barabbas, ____ Jesus who is called Christ?" (Matthew 27:17)

28 "Are You the ____ of the Jews?" (Matthew 27:11)

32 "Where did this Man get this wisdom and these ____ works?" (Matthew 13:54)

33 "Is it lawful to pay taxes to ____, or not?" (Matthew 22:17)

34 "How is it that you have ____ faith?" (Mark 4:40)

35 "What will a man give in ____ for his soul?" (Matthew 16:26)

36 "Who is greater, he who sits at the table, or he who ____?" (Luke 22:27)

38 "Who is this of whom I ____ such things?" (Luke 9:9)

40 "Why could we not ____ it out?" (Matthew 17:19)

42 "Where have you ____ him?" (John 11:34)

43 "Are you betraying the Son of Man with a ____?" (Luke 22:48)

44 "Could this be the Son of ____?" (Matthew 12:23)

45 "Are You greater than our father ____?" (John 8:53)

47 "Why this ____?" (Mattthew 26:8)

49 "The baptism of John—where was it from? From ____ or from men?" (Matthew 21:25)

53 "What further need do ____ have of witnesses?" (Matthew 26:65)

54 "Who can this be, that even the winds and the sea ____ Him?" (Matthew 8:27)

55 "Do men gather . . . ____ [sing.] from thistles?" (Matthew 7:16)

57 "How can this be, since I do not know a ____?" (Luke 1:34)

FISHERS OF MEN

Matthew 4:18 tells us that Jesus found Simon Peter and his brother Andrew fishing in the Sea of Galilee. Peter and Andrew were professional fishermen when Jesus called them to be His disciples. Fishing was all that they had known; it was quite possibly the only way they knew to make a living.

Jesus said to them, "Follow Me, and I will make you fishers of men" (v. 19). Jesus spoke in terms that they would understand. Indeed, so strong was the analogy for them, that the fish became the secret symbol identifying the early persecuted Christians.

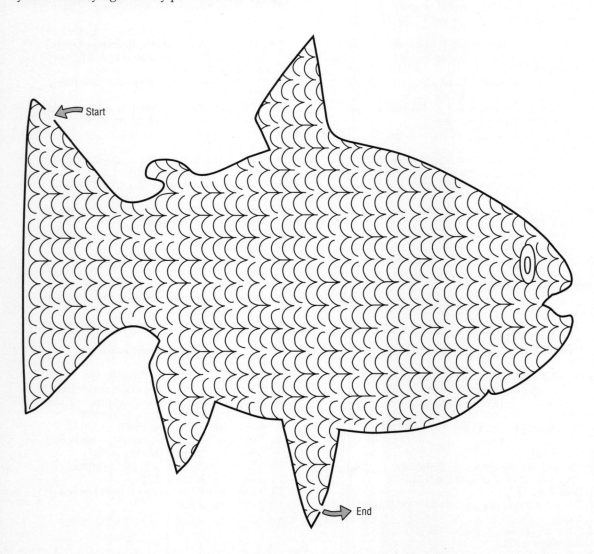

*W*hat is your first priority? What does the Scripture say it should be? To find out, unscramble the words and write them in the blank spaces.

ENTICINGARK — — — — — — — — — — — (2 words)

IYOUTHWIN — — — — — — — — (2 words)

SHAREENDUREDIT — — — — — — — — — — — — (2 words)

GRANTED — — — — — — —

WANDERLON — — — — — — — — —

YJO — — —

ASSUMEDTRED — — — — — — — — — — (2 words)

LAPPERFOGTARERICE — — — — — — — — — — — — — — — — — (4 words)

RAFASTERIMAGE — — — — — — — — — — (2 words)

SONGTHEUSESIR — — — — — — — — — — — —

PETREN — — — — — —

CEPEA — — — — —

VALENE — — — — — —

WROPE — — — — —

INVITEGNRS — — — — — — — — — — (2 words)

Unscrambled letters: — — — —   — — — — —

Scripture Pool

MATTHEW 3:2   MATTHEW 6:33   MATTHEW 13:31, 33, 44, 45–47   MATTHEW 18:23
MATTHEW 21:33   MATTHEW 22:2   MATTHEW 25:1   LUKE 17:21   ROMANS 14:17
1 CORINTHIANS 4:20

73

*H*is grace truly is amazing! Complete this grid with the words of one of the church's most famous hymns.

Stanza #1:

_____ _____, how sweet the _____
15 Across 18 Across   6 Down

That _____ a _____ _____ me!
    14 Down   12 Across   67 Down

I _____ was _____ , but now _____
  66 Across   13 Across   27 Across

_____ , Was _____, but _____ I see.
29 Down   21 Across   3 Down

Stanza #2:

_____ grace that taught _____ heart to
37 Across   63 Across

_____, And grace my _____ _____,
59 Down   2 Down   22 Across

How _____ _____ that grace _____
    34 Down   35 Down   39 Across

The _____ I _____ _____!
    9 Down   45 Across 7 Down

Stanza #3:

_____ many _____, _____ and _____,
49 Down   11 Down 49 Across   38 Down

I _____ _____ _____; _____ grace
  65 Down 50 Down 56 Down 43 Across

_____ _____ _____ _____ thus
41 Down 21 Down 63 Down 58 Across

_____, _____ grace will
2 Across 30 Across

_____ me _____.
23 Down and 67 Across   25 Across and 68 Across

Stanza #4:

The _____ has _____ _____ to _____,
    64 Across   51 Across 71 Across   69 Down

His _____ my _____ _____; He _____
    48 Down   5 Across 72 Across   61 Across

my _____ and _____ _____ As _____
  44 Across   36 Across 47 Across   62 Down

as life _____.
    4 Down

Stanza #5:

And when this _____ and _____ shall
      53 Across   32 Down

_____, And _____ _____ shall _____,
45 Down   1 Down   28 Across   33 Down

I shall _____ within the _____ A life of
    40 Down   20 Down

_____ and _____.
5 Across   19 Across

Stanza #6:

_____ we've been _____ _____ _____
57 Across   8 Down 8 Across 10 Across

_____, _____ _____ _____ the
70 Across 31 Across 26 Across 42 Down

_____, We've _____ _____ _____ to
16 Across   60 Across 64 Down 52 Down

_____ _____ _____ Than when _____
24 Down 54 Across 46 Down   73 Across

first _____.
  17 Down

To the Cave of Adullam

In escaping the jealous wrath of King Saul, David fled to the cave of Adullam. The Bible tells us, "When his brothers and all his father's house heard it, they went down there to him. And everyone who was in distress, everyone who was in debt, and everyone who was discontented gathered to him. So he became captain over them. And there were about four hundred men with him" (1 Samuel 22:1–2).

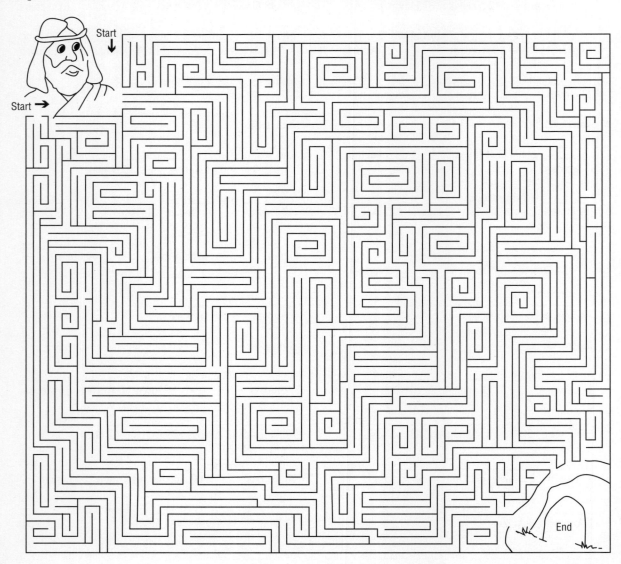

Unscramble these words that relate to the intimate, committed, steadfast, guiding, unending relationship the Lord has promised us. Then position the unscrambled words on the grid to reveal God's ultimate promise to us about that relationship.

DEBAI MIRSNTEEPNO SYAALW PNANIOMOC STTSEAADF
ROTREFMOC RREEEESNTPV (2 words) GNILRETSAVE ROVEREME
LNEETRA DEINRF VEROREF LOSENRUCO EHEPSRHD LSPITIRHYO (2 words)
MPENCSASO OCORETRTP REVILEDER HTGENRTS DNIKSESNGIOLVN (2 words)
TURHT VELO ENVI CEEPA CMOERVOE YUNOI (2 words)
DUOLCOLAFIRLP (3 words) ERFFORIALIPIL (3 words) GRLYOHANIKHSE (2 words) IDLEHS

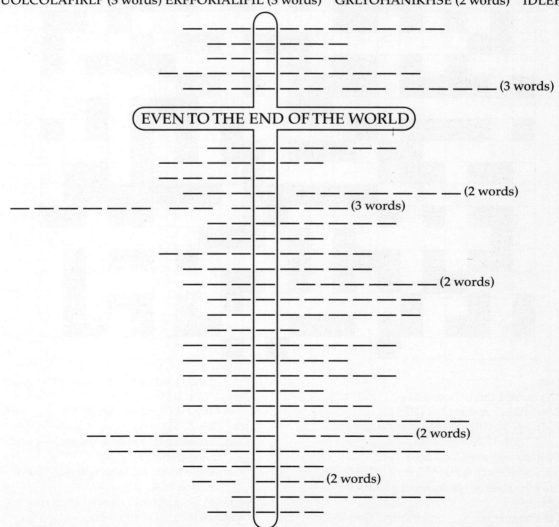

(3 words)

EVEN TO THE END OF THE WORLD

(2 words)

(3 words)

(2 words)

(2 words)

(2 words)

When Job lost everything he once owned and loved, he hurled bitter complaints and anguished accusations against God—the One he trusted and the One who could have prevented all his misery. But Job eventually came to recognize his shortsighted perspective and repented to the Lord. Job's ultimate comfort? God is sovereign.

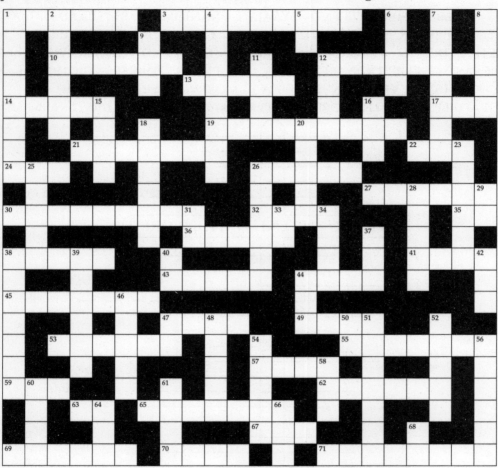

Across
1 Job owned three thousand _____ (Job 1:3)
3 Mourning apparel (Job 16:15)
10 "My eye has also grown dim because of _____" (Job 17:7)
12 Pottery fragment (Job 2:8)
13 This adversary accused Job of loving God only because of his material prosperity (Job 1:9)
14 "He hangs the _____ on nothing" (Job 26:7)
17 "_____ LORD gave, and _____ LORD has taken away" (Job 1:21)
19 "Till I die I will not put away my _____ from me" (Job 27:5)
21 God commended Job as a "blameless and _____ man" (Job 2:3)
22 "Cause me to understand wherein I have _____ed" (Job 6:24)
24 Job said his grief was heavier than the "sand of the _____ " (Job 6:3)

26 This adversity hit Job from head to foot (Job 2:7)
27 "My justice was like a robe and a ____" (Job 29:14)
30 "In this you are not ____" (Job 33:12)
32 "My ____ is a breath!" (Job 7:7)
35 There were "no women ____ beautiful as the daughters of Job" (Job 42:15)
36 "Who is this who darkens counsel by ____ without knowledge?" (Job 38:2)
38 Job's wife had this suggestion: "____ God and die" (Job 2:9)
41 "Stretch out your ____s toward Him" (Job 11:13)
43 "____ still and consider the wondrous works of God" (Job 37:14)
44 "Though He ____ me, yet will I trust Him" (Job 13:15)
45 "Remember to ____ His work" (Job 36:24)
47 "Have the ____s of death been revealed to you?" God asked Job (Job 38:17)
49 "Naked I came from my mother's ____, and naked shall I return" (Job 1:21)
53 "Therefore I . . . ____ in dust and ashes" (Job 42:6)
55 Job's friend, the Temanite (Job 4:1)
57 "My flesh is caked with ____s" (Job 7:5)
59 "Things ____ wonderful for me, which I did not know" (Job 42:3)
62 "Now . . . I will question you, and you shall ____ Me" (Job 38:3)
63 "____ at peace; Thereby good will come to you" (Job 22:21)
65 God "is excellent in power, in judgment and abundant ____" (Job 37:23)
67 Enclosure (abbr.)
69 "He has made me a ____ of the people" (Job 17:6)
70 What Job did to his robe when he heard about the death of his children (Job 1:20)
71 "I know that my ____ lives" (Job 19:25)

Down
1 "Shall the one who ____ with the Almighty correct Him?" (Job 40:2)
2 "See my ____!" (Job 10:15)
4 Adversity (Job 6:2)
5 "So Job died, old and full ____ days" (Job 42:17)
6 "He does great things ____ finding out" (Job 9:10)
7 "God is ____ than man" (Job 33:12)
8 Satan said God had a ____ around Job, protecting him (Job 1:10)
9 "In all this Job did ____ sin nor charge God with wrong" (Job 1:22)
11 "My righteousness I hold ____" (Job 27:6)
12 "Nor does He regard the rich more than the ____; for they are all the work of His hands" (Job 34:19)

15 "What strength do I have, that I should ____?" (Job 6:11)
16 Job's friends and relatives "came to him and ____ food with him" (Job 42:11)
18 "Where can ____ be found?" (Job 28:12)
20 "They saw that his ____ was very great" (Job 2:13)
23 "I desire to ____ with God" (Job 13:3)
25 The youngest of Job's four friends (Job 32:6)
26 One of Job's friends, a Shuhite (Job 8:1)
28 "You have not spoken of Me what is ____" (Job 42:7)
29 "Behold, God is mighty, but despises ____ one" (Job 36:5)
31 Southwest (abbr.)
33 "My spirit ____ broken, . . . the grave ____ ready for me" (Job 17:1)
34 "To depart from ____ is understanding" (Job 28:28)
37 Job "cursed the ____ of his birth" (Job 3:1)
38 "Miserable ____ers are you all!" (Job 16:2)
39 "Have I ____?" (Job 7:20)
40 Leviathan's "heart is ____ hard ____ stone" (Job 41:24)
42 "My speech settled on them as ____" (Job 29:22)
44 Job "____ his children and grandchildren for four generations" (Job 42:16)
46 "All ____ would perish together" (Job 34:15)
47 Great (abbr.)
48 In spite of his complaints, Job had great "confidence" in God (Job 13:15)
50 "The thing I greatly feared has come upon ____" (Job 3:25)
51 "____ be the name of the LORD" (Job 1:21)
52 "____ were you when I laid the foundations of the earth?" (Job 38:4)
54 God restored to Job "____ as much as he had before" (Job 42:10)
56 One of Job's comforters, a Naamathite (Job 11:1)
58 "What is ____?" (Job 7:17)
60 "If they ____ and serve Him, they shall spend their days in prosperity" (Job 36:11)
61 "I have become like ____ and ashes" (Job 30:19)
64 "Give ____, Job, listen to me" (Job 33:31)
66 "You have heard of the perseverance of Job and seen the ____ intended by the Lord—that the Lord is very compassionate and merciful" (James 5:11)
68 "____ who rebukes God, let him answer it" (Job 40:2)

A word for the mighty, the rich, and the wise.

Clue: **MESSIAH** *is* RUGGVIM

" WUD   MVR   NMQ   CWQEVUG

CWQES   VF   DMVG,'   DMID   MU

AFYUEGDIFYG   IFY

TFQNG   RU,'   DMID   VIR   DMU

WQEY,'   UOUEKVGVFC

WQLVFCTVFYFUGG,'

ZAYCRUFD,'   IFY

EVCMDUQAGFUGG   VF

DMU   UIEDM.   PQE   VF   DMUGU

V   YUWVCMD,'"   GISG

DMU   WQEY.

*S*even of the books in the New Testament were written by the apostle Paul to churches in cities in Europe and Asia Minor. Match the first half of the verse to the correct second half, then unscramble the circled letters in the correctly matched verses to reveal the city in which the church was located. When all the letters are in place, you will find the form in which these books were written.

Column A

1. For we are His workmanship,

2. Be anxious for nothing, but in everything by prayer and supplication, with thanksgiving,

3. Therefore, if anyone is in Christ, he is a new creation;

4. For in Him dwells all the fullness of the Godhead bodily;

5. I have been crucified with Christ; it is no longer I who live, but Christ lives in me;

6. And may the Lord make you increase and abound in love to one another and to all, just as we do to you,

7. For I am not ashamed of the gospel of Christ, for it is the power of God to salvation for everyone who believes, for the Jew first and also for the Greek.

Column B

A. and you are complete in Him, who is the head of all principality and power.

B. so that He may establish your hearts blameless in holiness before our God and Father at the coming of our Lord Jesus Christ with all His saints.

C. created in Christ Jesus for good works, which God prepared beforehand that we should walk in them.

D. Let your requests be made known to God.

E. old things have passed away; behold, all things have become new.

F. For in it the righteousness of God is revealed from faith to faith; as it is written, "The just shall live by faith."

G. and the life which I now live in the flesh I live by faith in the Son of God, who loved me and gave Himself for me.

Unscrambled Letters:

1. __ __ __ __ __ __ __

2. __ __ __ __ __ __ __ __

3. __ __ __ __ __ __ __

4. __ __ __ __ __ __ __

5. __ __ __ __ __ __ __

6. __ __ __ __ __ __ __ __ __ __

7. __ __ __ __ __

Match:

1 - _____

2 - _____

3 - _____

4 - _____

5 - _____

6 - _____

7 - _____

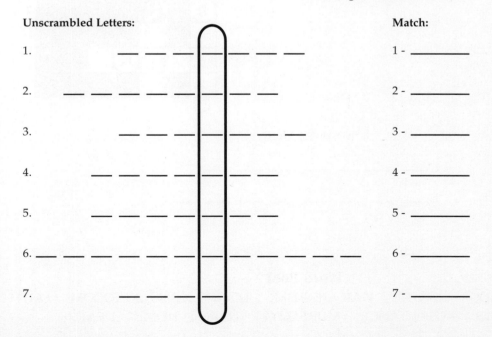

*B*elow is a Word Pool containing two separate sets of words—but the words are all mixed up together. To divide the words into their proper categories, put each word in its correct place on the correct grid. When you unscramble the circled letters you will see how the words are related—and how the sets are opposite!

1.

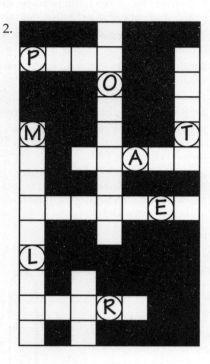

2.

Unscrambled letters:

1. __ __ __ __ __ __ __

2. __ __ __ __ __ __ __ __

Word Pool

LIFE   KNOWLEDGE   TRUTH   WAR   FATHER   LOVE   PAIN   KINGDOM   FAITH

TONGUES   INHERITANCE   MORTALITY   TEARS   HOME   DEATH

The answer to each definition in the first column is contained within one of the names in the second column. The hidden word will be found with its letters in correct order. An example is given for you.

1. __Y__ Large	A.	Issachar
2. ____ Melody	B.	Philistines
3. ____ Praise	C.	Alphaeus
4. ____ Disturbance	D.	Aristarchus
5. ____ Burn	E.	Tabitha
6. ____ Male swan	F.	Candace
7. ____ Food shop	G.	Claudius Caesar
8. ____ Bridle	H.	Artaxerxes
9. ____ Tease	I.	Amalekites
10. ____ Pain	J.	Potiphar
11. ____ Edging	K.	Agrippa
12. ____ Get up	L.	Rachel
13. ____ Citrus	M.	Apollos
14. ____ Gratuity	N.	Nehemiah
15. ____ Roster	O.	David
16. ____ Levy	P.	Timothy
17. ____ Liturgy	Q.	Iscariot
18. ____ Survey	R.	Pharisees
19. ____ Stiffen	S.	Amorites
20. ____ Mountain	T.	Delilah
21. ____ Top quality	U.	Agabus
22. ____ Child's toy	V.	Sennacherib
23. ____ Insect	W.	Philemon
24. ____ Transport	X.	Jacob
25. ____ Hold tightly	➔ Y.	Abigail
26. ____ Eager	Z.	Zacharias

HEARING WITH THE HEART

Matthew 13:10–17 gives us an indication of the importance Christ placed on *hearing* the Word of God. In this passage, Jesus' disciples ask why He speaks to the people in parables. He responds that the people have heard the Scriptures but do not understand them. He speaks to them in a way that they both hear and understand *in their hearts.* Hearing the Word is important for convincing the heart of truth.

Start at the top left corner and go to the heart at the bottom of the page. To get there, cross through words only having to do with sounds, hearing, or messages. Do not cross through corners. Move only to a word that shares a line with the current word.

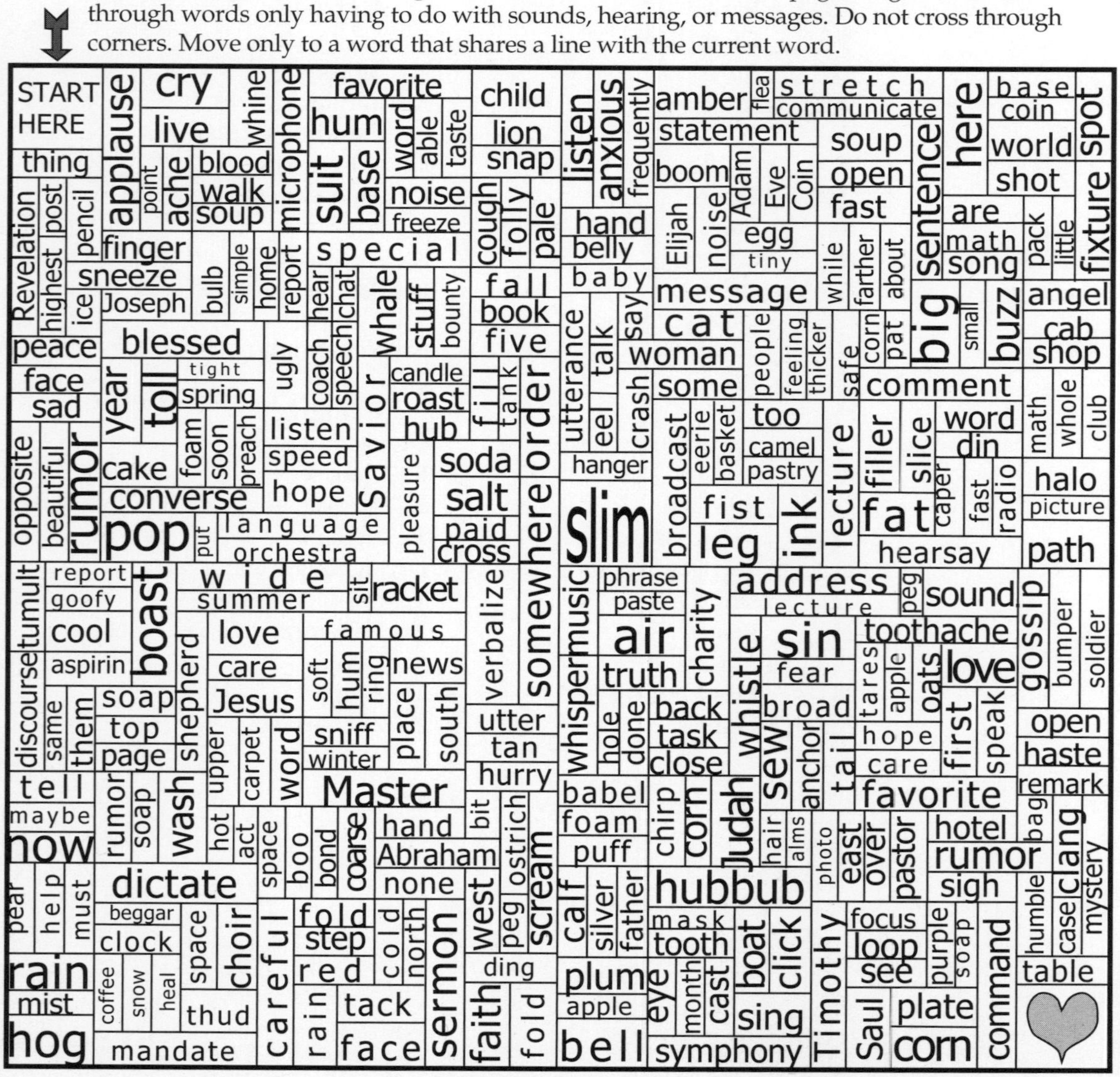

[A large word-grid puzzle fills the lower portion of the page. The grid begins at "START HERE" in the top-left corner and ends at a heart symbol in the bottom-right corner. The grid contains hundreds of words including: cry, favorite, child, amber, stretch, base, applause, live, whine, hum, word, lion, listen, anxious, statement, soup, here, coin, world, spot, thing, blood, walk, suit, noise, boom, open, fast, are, shot, fixture, finger, special, cough, hand, egg, song, math, pencil, sneeze, report, home, stuff, fall, baby, message, cat, buzz, angel, Joseph, speech, whale, book, five, woman, some, big, cab, shop, peace, blessed, candle, roast, utterance, talk, too, comment, word, din, halo, face, sad, year, toll, listen, speed, hub, soda, order, hanger, broadcast, camel, lecture, slice, filler, fat, picture, opposite, rumor, converse, hope, Savior, salt, paid, cross, slim, fist, leg, ink, hearsay, path, pop, language, orchestra, pleasure, report, wide, racket, verbalize, somewhere, phrase, paste, address, sound, gossip, goofy, summer, sit, music, lecture, peg, cool, love, famous, air, charity, sin, toothache, love, bumper, soldier, aspirin, care, news, truth, fear, oats, soap, Jesus, soft, hum, ring, place, south, utter, whisper, done, back, whistle, broad, first, speak, open, top, page, sniff, winter, tan, hurry, hope, care, haste, remark, tell, Master, word, babel, corn, Judah, sew, anchor, favorite, hotel, clang, now, hand, foam, chirp, hair, alms, photo, east, over, pastor, rumor, mystery, dictate, Abraham, none, puff, hubbub, sigh, humble, case, help, must, beggar, coarse, scream, calf, silver, father, mask, tooth, focus, loop, purple, soap, table, rain, clock, choir, fold, step, cold, north, sermon, west, peg, ostrich, ding, boat, click, Timothy, see, plate, command, mist, coffee, snow, heal, space, red, rain, tack, faith, fold, plume, apple, eye, month, cast, sing, Saul, corn, hog, mandate, thud, careful, face, bell, symphony]

God has made Himself known to us. Unscramble the letters below and discover some of the ways that God has told us—*and tells us*—about Himself. The circled letters will spell out a word that means what God has made known to us. The second set of scrambled letters makes words that tell us what we are to do with what God has told us. The circled letters spell a word that tells us what we are to *be* with what God has told us.

DROW (1 Samuel 3:21)   — — — —

SEUSJ (Galatians 1:12)   — — — — —

SHAVENE (Psalm 19:1)   — — — — — — —

POETSPHR (Amos 3:7)   — — — — — — — —

SPOGEL (Romans 1:16–17)   — — — — — —

REACTION (Romans 1:19–21)   — — — — — — — —

HERAFT (Matthew 11:25; 16:17)   — — — — — —

TRIPIS (1 Corinthians 2:10)   — — — — — —

KROWS (John 10:25)   — — — — —

TWINESEYES (2 Peter 1:16)   — — — — — — — — — —

WAKENMONK (Psalm 145:12)   — — — —   — — — — —   (2 words)

MIRACLOP (Isaiah 61:1)   — — — — — — — —

LELT (Mark 5:19)   — — — —

NEHIS (Philippians 2:15)   — — — — —

PORTER (1 Corinthians 14:25)   — — — — — —

PAKES (Titus 2:15)   — — — — —

SERAPI (Psalm 145:4)   — — — — — —

REDLACE (1 Chronicles 16:24)   — — — — — — —

FEISTTY (1 Peter 5:12)   — — — — — — —

PUZZLE ANSWERS

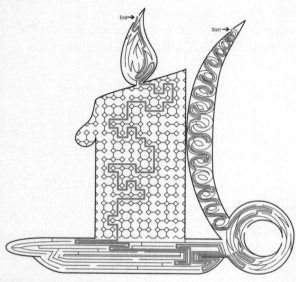

1 — C, Romans 6:17
2 — G, 1 Peter 1:22
3 — E, Romans 5:19
4 — B, Deuteronomy 13:4
5 — F, 1 Samuel 15:22
6 — A, John 14:23
7 — D, Jeremiah 7:23

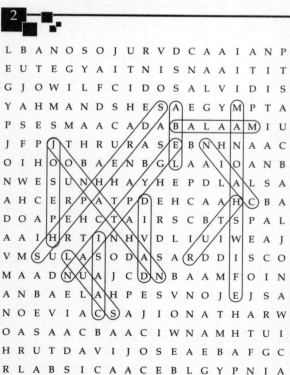

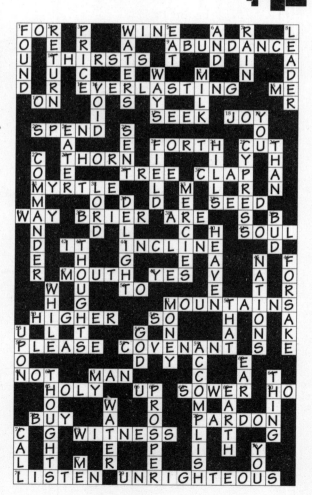

5

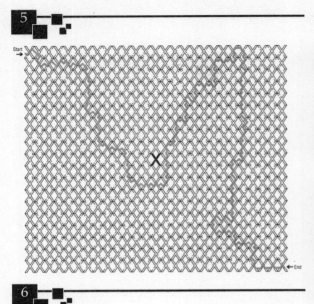

Start →

← End

7

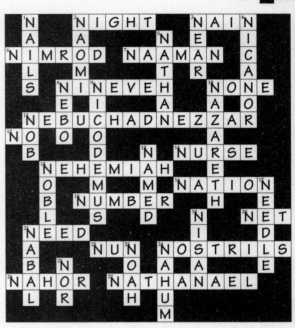

6

VINE
FRUIT
TEND
KEEPERS
SPICED WINE
BRANCHES
OWNER
CLUSTERS
BLOSSOMS
PRUNE
GRAPES

VINEDRESSER

8

Puzzle Answers

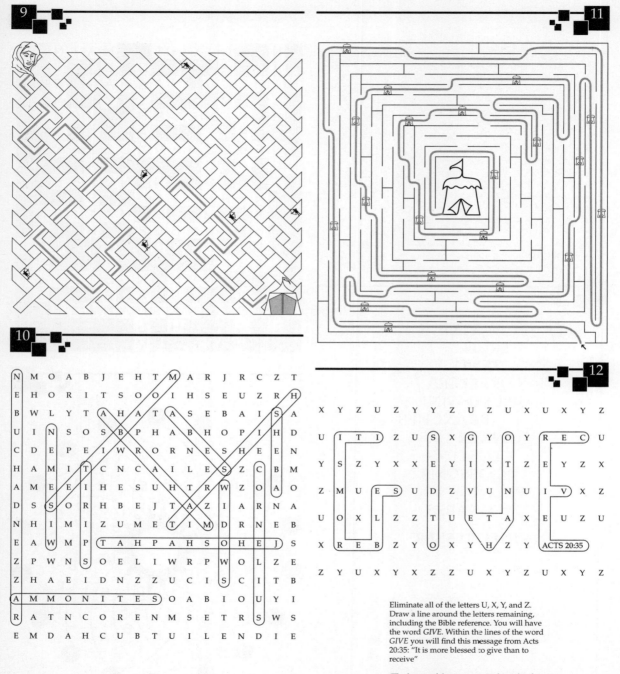

9

10

11

12

Eliminate all of the letters U, X, Y, and Z. Draw a line around the letters remaining, including the Bible reference. You will have the word *GIVE*. Within the lines of the word *GIVE* you will find this message from Acts 20:35: "It is more blessed to give than to receive"

(The letters of the verse are in the order they would be in if you were writing the word *GIVE*.)

13

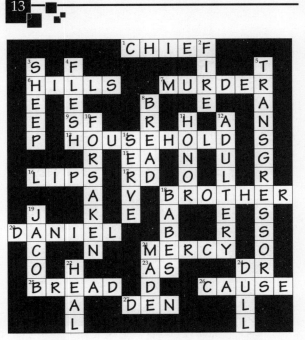

15

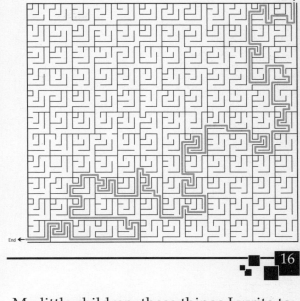

16

My little children, these things I write to you, so that you may not sin. And if anyone sins, we have an Advocate with the Father, Jesus Christ the righteous. And He Himself is the propitiation for our sins, and not for ours only but also for the whole world. (1 John 2:1–2)

14

```
G Z I O L I B A L I G O B H B A
I S O S B E O D E A M E R O N L
L E N I A T A A B E D T L I A E
B V L N R H L O M O R I A S I B
A I A A E O I A V S G O I G O L
L C R L C R C R E G E R I Z I M
E B I O A E L M I Z A R E P V S
A G C L M B E L A I G B Z I A R
L A A I S S E I R L O D R S P E
R I R V E A B A A B A E A G I P
M O M N D I N M R D A N A G I
P I E O L S E R A O L O N H M R
E Z L I R O B A T V M B M E N O
R A O Z A I L Z S R A L A B B M
A L M C R M A I E E N I Z I G O
M B R O L E N H V S I G T E T H
E E A M E A L E M E S B A S A E
R A H N I S A D O R S O R H R R
A E R I O L I G L I A C I A S M
T E V R L C M O I Z V E R O R O
```

19

He who does not love Me does not keep My words; and the word which you hear is not Mine but the Father's who sent Me. (John 14:24)

20

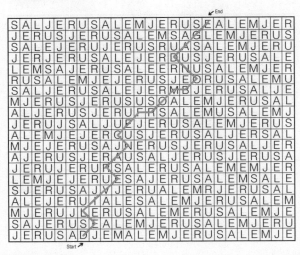

21

Let not your heart be troubled; you believe in God, believe also in Me. (John 14:1)

22

BAT**H**SHEBA
R**A**CHEL
ZI**P**PORAH
ZIL**P**AH
MAR**Y**
BASE**M**ATH
J**O**CHEBED
RU**T**H
LEA**H**
EVE
HAGA**R**
SARAH
A**D**AH
H**A**NNAH
MAR**Y**

HAPPY MOTHER'S DAY

23

Bonus: HEAVEN

PUZZLE ANSWERS

24

26

Bonus: SEVENTH DAY

25

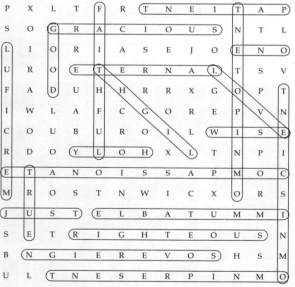

27

SIL**A**S
MARK
TIM**O**THY
TYRA**N**NUS
A**G**ABUS
EU**T**YCHUS
TYC**H**ICUS
AEN**E**AS
LUK**E**
G**A**IUS
DAMA**R**IS
LYDIA
MAR**Y**
PRIS**C**ILLA
TROP**H**IMUS
E**R**ASTUS
AQU**I**LA
ARI**S**TARCHUS
TABI**T**HA
S**I**LVANUS
SOP**A**TER
COR**N**ELIUS
ONE**S**IMUS

AMONG THE EARLY CHRISTIANS

28

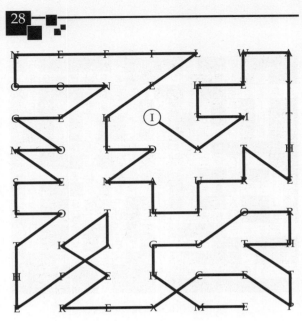

I am the way, the truth, and the life. No one comes to the Father except through Me. (John 14:6)

30

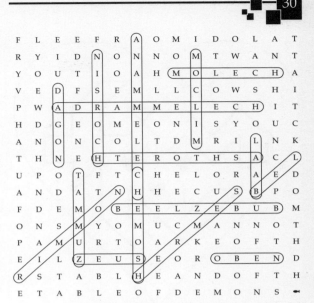

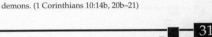

Flee from idolatry… I do not want you to have fellowship with demons. You cannot drink the cup of the Lord and the cup of demons; you cannot partake of the Lord's table and of the table of demons. (1 Corinthians 10:14b, 20b–21)

29

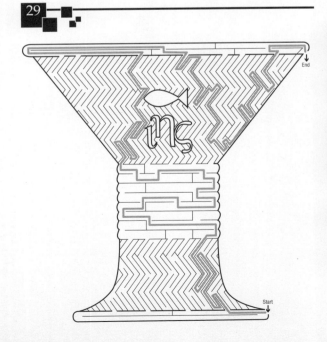

31

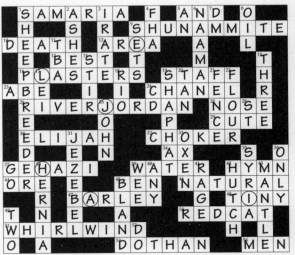

Bonus: ELIJAH

Puzzle Answers

He who does not love does not know
God, for God is love. (1 John 4:8)

Bonus: PROMISED LAND

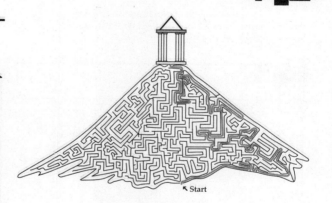

36

```
L C N T U S N O I T N E T N O C I E E
E L E R N S Y M O I S R S S M R B W A
N N A E O E R F U N S O O U T M C D B
V E R C T N M O U R E R R N K E N E U
E S E I A N U R D C D D U C S S E N R
R S V O L E L N E I E D R I E H A H T
E H E N O K E I S R F I S H A R D T S
H O L S D N W C S A O D Y S E E Y A R
E D R I A U D A H T R E R V R Y V R T
W U I T Y R E T L U D A T T N D N W F
U T E S R D F I B F N N A R I E E F O
B B S J S W O O U L I H L S W I S O L
T U R S T E S N R E C N O T E N N S F
U O S L E A N T S S A S D V Y T O T H
E E S E L F I S H A M B I T I O N S R
R S I W L O E U I O T O S O D I S R R
I D E D M I W S I O I S N W B T E U L
S Y N N S E D S R S N S T A M S E B S
I V L E L U O L A E J S H S I E S T W
D S R S S I D S S E N N A E L C N U D
S E E S N J E A L O U S I E S T N O C
H N N A I O N S S E M U R U N C O L E
```

37

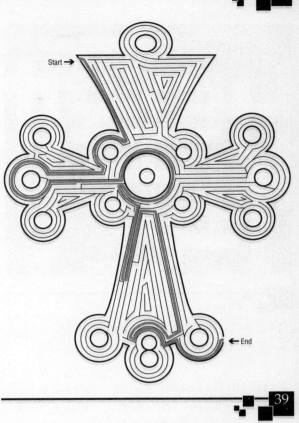

Start →

← End

38

39

NOT **P**ARADE ITSELF
ABID**E**
ENDU**R**ES
NOT PU**F**FED UP
NOT **E**NVY
NOT REJOI**C**E IN INIQUITY
GREA**T**EST
BE**L**IEVES
THINKS N**O** EVIL
NOT PRO**V**OKED
THERE IS NO F**E**AR IN LOVE. BUT…
BE**C**AME A MAN
NOT BEH**A**VE RUDELY
NOT **S**EEK ITS OWN
FACE **T**O FACE
IS KIND
H**O**PES
S**U**FFERS
TRUTH
NEVER **F**AILS
P**E**RFECT
AS I **A**LSO AM KNOWN
BEA**R**S

There is no fear in love; but perfect love
casts out fear. (1 John 4:18)

Crossword (37)

	1 A	2 P	3 O		4 O	5 F	F		6 C	7 S	8 L		9 S
10	E	X	A	M	11 P	L	E		12 C	H	O	O	S	E
14	T	A		15 R	E	A	D		16 S	H	E	L	T	I	E
17 S	E	R	V	A	N	T		19 T	H	E	R	E		20 L	M
21 H	A	T	E	D			22 H	E	R	O	D			24 S	O	S
25 O	C	H	R	E		26 C	U	R	D	S			A		R
27 W	H	E	Y		28 P	R	O	T	E	A			29 L	E	I
	N			L		30 N	H		R			V		G
31 O		32 P		33 A	E	R	O		34 S		35 S	M	A	S	37 H
38 P	R	O	C	L	A	I	M		A		40 M	O	T	E	T
E		41 T	O	A	S	T	I	N	42 G		43 A	S	I	A
N			44 G	R	E	E	C	E		45 A	L	S	O
46 S	P	A	S	M		47 S	T	E	A	L		48 N	O	R

PUZZLE ANSWERS

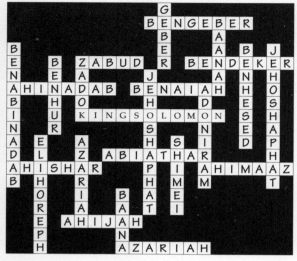

JUST ONE
WOND**E**RFUL
SERVANT
OUR RIGHTEO**U**SNESS
COUN**S**ELOR
KING OF **T**HE JEWS
C**H**RIST
VIN**E**
ALPHA AND O**M**EGA
PRINCE OF P**E**ACE
MAN OF **S**ORROWS
DAY**S**PRING
MED**I**ATOR
BRIGHT **A**ND MORNING STAR
SHEP**H**ERD

JESUS THE MESSIAH

43

Come to Me, all you who labor and are heavy laden, and I will give you rest. Take My yoke upon you and learn from Me, for I am gentle and lowly in heart, and you will find rest for your souls. For My yoke is easy and My burden is light. (Matthew 11:28–30)

Blood	Pestilence	Locusts
Frogs	Boils	Darkness
Lice	Hail	Death
Flies		

Unscrambled letters: HARDENED HEART

45

47

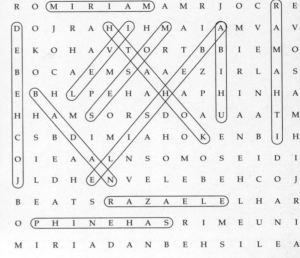

Levi—great-grandfather; Kohath—grandfather;
Amram—father; Jochebed—mother;
Moses—brother; Miriam—sister; Elisheba—wife;
Nadab, Abihu, Eleazar, Ithamar—sons;
Phinehas—grandson

46

$$30{,}000 \times 0.25 \div 480 \times 4 \times 60 \div 3 \times 20$$
$$- 3{,}300 \div 20 \times 2 - 2{,}000 + 40 \div 30 = 7$$

48

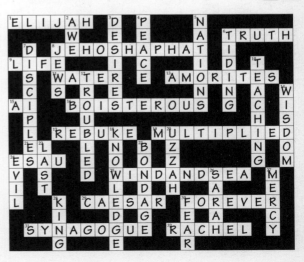

PUZZLE ANSWERS

JACOB   ELIJAH
NOAH   children of REUBEN and GAD
ABRAHAM   LEVITES
MOSES

Unscrambled letters: ALTAR

In every place where I record My name I will come to you, and I will bless you. (Exodus 20:24)

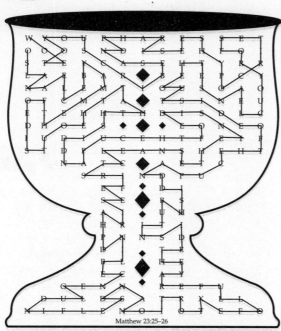

Matthew 23:25–26

Woe to you, scribes and Pharisees, hypocrites! For you cleanse the outside of the cup and dish, but inside they are full of extortion and self-indulgence. Blind Pharisee, first cleanse the inside of the cup and dish, that the outside of them may be clean also. (Matthew 23:25–26)

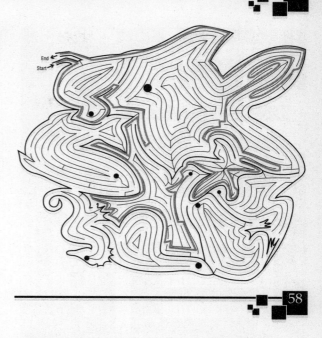

Rejoice always, pray without ceasing, in every-thing give thanks; for this is the will of God in Christ Jesus for you. (1 Thessalonians 5:16–18)

$$144,000 \div 20,000,000 \times 7,000 - 4 \div 2 \times 5 + 24 \div 7 + 1 \div 3 = 7$$

PUZZLE ANSWERS

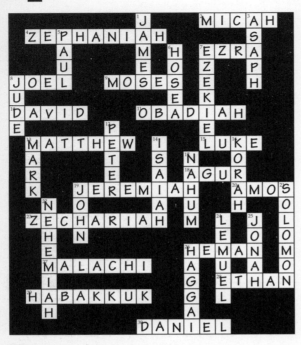

WHITE	BLUE	GOLDEN
BLACK	PALE	YELLOW
GREEN	RED	BROWN
CRIMSON	SCARLET	GRAY
PURPLE		

Unscrambled letters: TUNIC
STONES
EAGLE

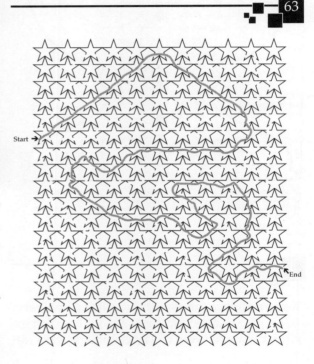

63

60

Be strong and of good courage; do not be afraid, nor be dismayed, for the LORD your God is with you wherever you go. (Joshua 1:9)

61

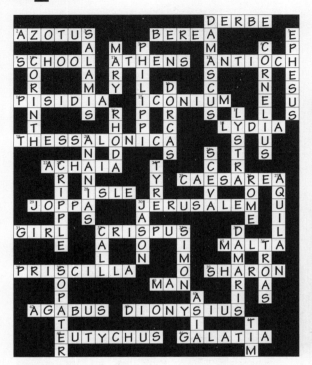

Let not your heart be troubled; you believe in God, believe also in Me. (John 14:1)

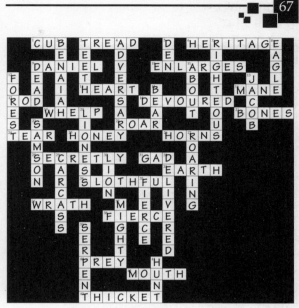

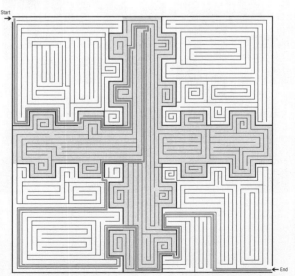

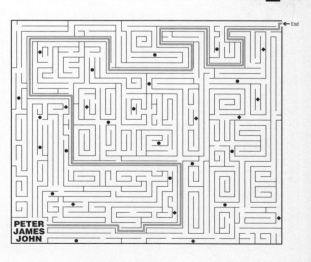

67

PETER
JAMES
JOHN

69

These things I have written to you who believe in the name of the Son of God, that you may know that you have eternal life, and that you may continue to believe in the name of the Son of God. (1 John 5:13)

70

71

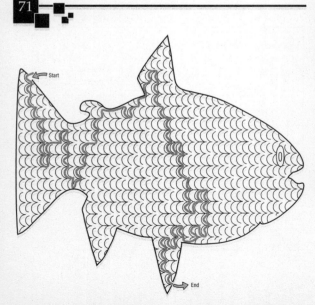

Start

End

72

CERTAIN **KING**
WITHIN **YOU**
HIDDEN **T**REASURE
DRAGNET
LANDOWNER
JOY
MUSTARD SEED

PEARL **OF** GREAT PRICE
MARRIAGE **F**EAST

RIGHTEOUSNESS
REP**E**NT
PEACE
LEA**V**EN
POWER
TEN VIRGINS

Unscrambled letters: SEEK FIRST

73

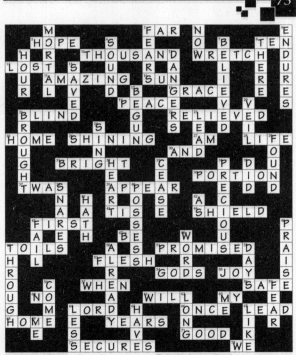

Amazing grace, how sweet the sound
That saved a wretch like me!
I once was lost, but now am found,
Was blind, but now I see.

'Twas grace that taught my heart to fear,
And grace my fears relieved;
How precious did that grace appear
The hour I first believed!

Through many dangers, toils, and snares,
I have already come;
'Tis grace hath brought me safe thus far,
And grace will lead me home.

The Lord had promised good to me,
His word my hope secures;
He will my shield and portion be
As long as life endures.

And when this flesh and heart shall fail,
And mortal life shall cease,
I shall possess within the veil
A life of joy and peace.

When we 've been there ten thousand years,
Bright shining as the sun,
We've no less days to sing God's praise
Than when we first begun.

Crossword grid (76):

C A M E L S · S A C K C L O T H · P · G · H
O · I · N · A · F · · · R · A · E
N · S O R R O W · L · F · P O T S H E R D
T · E · T · S A T A N · O · S · A · G
E A R T H · M · S · O · A · T H E
N · Y · O · I N T E G R I T Y · E · E R R
D · U P R I G H T · R · E · R · E
S E A · E · S D · Y · B O I L S · E
L · E · D · I · E · T U R B A N
R I G H T E O U S · L I F E · I · S O
O · M · W O R D S · V · D · G · O
C U R S E · A · A · I · A · H A N D
O · I · · S T A N D · S L A Y · T · E W
M A G N I F Y · A · · W O M B · W
F · N L · G A T E · · · · · W
O · R E P E N T · R · T · E L I P H A Z
R · D · S H · R · E · O
T O O · H · D · U · W O R M · E · P
B · B E · J U S T I C E · N · S E · H A
Y W O R D · T O R E · D · R E D E E M E R

Unscrambled words:
ABIDE OMNIPRESENT ALWAYS COMPAINION
STEADFAST COMFORTER EVER PRESENT EVERLASTING
EVERMORE ETERNAL FREIND FOREVER COUNSELOR
SHEPHERD HOLY SPIRIT ENCOMPASS PROTECTOR
DELIVERER STRENGTH LOVINGKINDNESS
TRUTH LOVE VINE PEACE OVERCOME
IN YOU PILLAR OF CLOUD PILLAR OF FIRE
SHEKINAH GLORY SHIELD

OMNIPRESENT
ALWAYS
SHIELD
EVERLASTING
PILLAR OF FIRE
EVEN TO THE END OF THE WORLD
EVERMORE
FOREVER
ABIDE
EVER PRESENT
PILLAR OF CLOUD
SHEPHERD
PEACE
DELIVERER
STRENGTH
HOLY SPIRIT
PROTECTOR
COUNSELOR
VINE
ENCOMPASS
ETERNAL
COMFORTER
LOVE
OVERCOME
STEADFAST
SHEKINAH GLORY
LOVINGKINDNESS
FRIEND
IN YOU
COMPANION
TRUTH

I WILL NEVER LEAVE YOU NOR FORSAKE YOU

"Let him who glories glory in this, that he understands and knows Me, that I am the LORD, exercising lovingkindness, judgment, and righteousness in the earth. For in these I delight," says the LORD" (Jeremiah 9:24)

Match 1-C (Ephesians 2:10), 2-D (Philippians 4:6), 3-E (2 Corinthians 5:17), 4-A (Colossians 2:9–10), 5-G (Galatians 2:20), 6-B (1 Thessalonians 3:12-13), 7-F (Romans 1:16–17)

EPHESUS
PHILIPPI
CORINTH
COLOSSE
GALATIA
THESSALONICA
ROME
EPISTLE

PUZZLE ANSWERS

Unscrambled letters:
1. ETERNAL
2. TEMPORAL

All the items in the first grid are eternal;
the items in the second grid are temporal.

1. Y. Abigail
2. Z. Zacharias
3. G. Claudius Caesar
4. Q. Iscariot
5. A. Issachar
6. X. Jacob
7. T. Delilah
8. E. Tabitha
9. V. Sennacherib
10. L. Rachel
11. N. Nehemiah
12. R. Pharisees
13. W. Philemon
14. J. Potiphar
15. B. Philistines
16. H. Artaxerxes
17. S. Amorites
18. M. Apollos
19. D. Aristarchus
20. C. Alphaeus
21. F. Candace
22. I. Amalekites
23. P. Timothy
24. U. Agabus
25. K. Agrippa
26. O. David

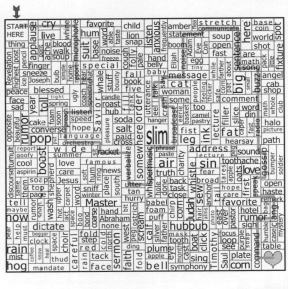

WORD
JESUS
HEAVENS
PROPHETS
GOSPEL
CREATION
FATHER
SPIRIT
WORKS
EYEWITNESS

REVELATION

MAKE KNOWN
PROCLAIM
TELL
SHINE
REPORT
SPEAK
PRAISE
DECLARE
TESTIFY

WITNESSES